Militärfahrzeuge

of the WEHRMACHT

VOLUME 2

Panzerkampfwagen III flying the standard of the battalion command. It is flanked by Pz.Kpfw.
IV Ausf. F/2, Pz.Kpfw. II and several m.S.P.W. Sd.Kfz. 251.

Militärfahrzeuge
of the
WEHRMACHT

Robert Johnson

Kurt Rieger and Uwe Feist

VOLUME 2

RYTON PUBLICATIONS

Militärfahrzeuge of the Wehrmacht

Copyright © **2004** by FEIST PUBLICATIONS

Designed by Uwe Feist
Artwork by Uwe Feist

Published by RYTON PUBLICATIONS U.S.A
P.O. Box 2306
Bellingham, WA 98227

ISBN - 1 - 930-571-32-1

Photo Credit:

Uwe Feist Collection
Kurt Rieger
Ryan E. Abbott
Bob Fleming Panzer Prints
Walter J. Spielberger
George Petersen
Fred Charlton Archive
Bruce Culver Collection
Wolfgang Fleischer
APG Museum
Patton Museum
Panzermuseum Munster

Printed in Korea by Tara TPS

Contents

Introduction

German tanks entered the annals of armored warfare for the first time on March 21, 1918 at St.Quentin, France. A group of five A7V Sturmpanzerkampfwagen accompanied by five captured British Mark IV achieved some local success against British infantry.

In total, a mere twenty A7V were built, compared to the 2,850 tanks built by the British until November 1918.

After the last shots of World War II (1939-1945) in Europe rang out, and the Armored Fighting Vehicle (AFV) was left abandoned by its crew, the legendary German "Panzertruppe" had forever left their brand in the history of war. Hundreds of concepts of Panzerkampfwagen had been conceived in the design departments of German companies such as Krupp, Rheinmetall-Borsig, MAN, Daimler-Benz, Henschel and the Czech firms of Skoda and BMM. Opel AG and Ford, due to their American affiliation, were excluded from armor development.

Prototypes of experimental tanks were secretly constructed as early as 1926; Krupp, Daimler and Rheinmetall developed vehicles under the code name "Grosstraktor".

The Panzerkampfwagen (MG) 1, Ausführung A (Sd.Kfz.101) was introduced to the public during a grand parade for Reichskanzler Adolf Hitler's 47th birthday on 20. April, 1936 in Berlin. The Pz.Kpfw.I and Pz.Kpfw.II were originally intended as training vehicles. They were armed with twin 7,92mm MG 13, later MG 34 machine guns for the Pz.Kpfw.1 and a 2cm KwK 30 with co-axial MG 34 in the turret of the Panzerkampfwagen II. Both vehicles were built in great numbers and played a major role in Germany's early military development.

Four Panzerbattalione equipped with Pz.Kpfw.I Ausf.A and Ausf.B were sent to Spain in 1936 as part of the famous "Legion Condor" in support of Generalissimo Franco's army of liberation against the Soviet backed Republican forces. The surviving armored vehicles remained in Spain after the Legion withdrew in 1939. Germany occupied Czechoslovakia in 1939 and confiscated a large number of tanks. The approximately 300 Skoda built Lt 35 were redesignated Panzerkampfwagen 35(t). Also, the BMM-built TNH tank was renamed Panzerkampfwagen 38(t). Both were welcome additions to the growing Panzertruppe of the late 1930's.

The 16 to mittlerer Panzerkampfwagen III (3,7cm) medium tank and the Panzerkampfwagen IV (7,5cm) soon replaced the light tanks, whose obsolete chassis were converted into self-propelled guns or rebuilt as tank destroyers.

A good number of captured French and British AFVs found use in the fast expanding Ostheer and were modified or rebuilt into 511 self-propelled gun carriages.

The campaign against the Soviet Union in June 1941, which the German army entered with 3,100 Panzerfahrzeuge of which 965 were Panzer III and 439 Panzer IV, soon revealed serious shortcomings regarding firepower, armor protection and mobility. This was especially the case when confronting the new Russian tank types, such as the medium T-34/76 and the heavy KVI tanks.

The Pz.Kpfw. VI TIGER I and the 7,5cm Pz.Kpfw.V PANTHER gave the Germans, once again, an edge over their adversary.

Always outnumbered by allied armor, the Germans attempted parity with highly specialized training in tactics and techniques. Tank crews were turned out from the "Panzerschulen" (tank schools) in less than 120 days. In addition, Germany increasingly relied on their excellent assault guns and tank destroyers, based on the proven Panzer III and IV chassis, as they were forced into the defensive on all fronts.

The Sturmgeschütz took a heavy toll of enemy armor. By spring 1944 the 20,000th Russian AFV fell victim to the "Sturmgeschütz". A single Stu.G Brigade, consisting of not more than 20 operational vehicles, knocked out 1,000 tanks in 15 months. But the powerful TIGER II, the tank hunters "ELEFANT" and "JAGDTIGER", built only in small numbers, could not alter the outcome of the conflict. When the final tally was taken, 23,487 tanks and 42,932 fully tracked self-propelled guns were produced and deployed between 1939 and 1945. On the opposite side an estimated 100,000 Russian AFVs lay burned out all over Russia and Eastern Europe. The Russians, Americans, and British built approximately 212,000 tanks, almost a ratio of 1:10.

The War in the East was very costly in men and material for both sides. Records show the loss of German AFVs from December 1, 1943 until November 30, 1944: Panzer IV, approximately 2,450; Pz.Kpfw.V PANTHER, approximately 2,130; Tiger I and Tiger II, approximately 540; Stu.G III, approximately 2,350. However many vehicles would be repaired and put into action again. The battles were fierce and towards the end the greatest production potential played as important a role as performance and fighting skill.

Eighty-seven years after the end of World War I, all that remains of the awesome armor armada from both conflicts are a few veterans on display in military museums and several thousand documented photographs - the only remaining visual records of a force that shaped the world.

6

Belgium, May 1940. Pz.Kpfw. I and Pz.Kpfw. II of 4. Panzer Division during the XVI Korps advance toward the Gembloux Gap. The heavier Pz.Kpfw. IV lead the formation in the distance.

TANK DEVELOPMENTS DURING THE "REICHSWEHR" PERIOD

The fact that the Treaty of Versailles explicitly banned any research on armored vehicles, created a vacuum within the German Army, which many of the responsible officers did not seem to be able to tolerate. Intensive studies of foreign developments led to certain ideas which found their way to reality through various prototypes. Designed and built under utmost secrecy, some of them were transferred to Russia, where Germany maintained a testing station near Kazan. Early self-propelled mount developments by Rheinmetall, Unterlüss utilized the standard 3.7 cm Kwk gun. They were fitted under partial armor to a Hanomag commercial tractor chassis. One hundred thirty-eight of these "3.7 cm WD-Schlepper 25 PS" were to be procured as equipment for anti-tank units. Also in 1927, trials began with the heavier Hanomag model in mounting a 7.7 cm gun for infantry support. They were called "7.7 cm WD-Schlepper 50 PS". Both systems were field-tested but not accepted.

The light tank design started in 1928 when Waffenamt ordered both Krupp and Rheinmetall to build the "Leichttraktor". Each company produced three prototypes, two each as battle tanks, while the third vehicle was to be developed as a supply vehicle or a self-propelled mount. Rheinmetall's design was a full-tracked 8.5 ton vehicle with a crew of four. 13 mm armor plate was provided, while the fully-rotating turret mounted a 3.7 cm Flak L/45 and one MG. Field trials started in 1930. It was intended to originally equip one light tank company with 17 of these vehicles and a total production of 289 "Leichttraktor" was anticipated. Nineteen hundred and thirty-two already had revealed that the basic concept could not be accepted, since the vehicles did not meet the necessary requirements. To shorten development time, and to catch up with the progress other nations had made in the design of tanks, the idea was entertained to purchase a Carden-Loyd

Krupp Leichttraktor.

The 9 t Rheinmetall-Leichttraktor 3,7cm Kanone L/45 with co-axial MG 13.

The second of only two Rheinmetall-Borsig Grosstraktor "Heavy Tractor" prototype vehicles.

The prototype for the Panzerkampfwagen III, the Z.W. (Zugführerwagen) by the Firma Krupp-Essen.

chassis from England, which was to serve as a basis for future developments. This resulted in the production in 1933 of the "Landwirtschaftliche Schlepper", better known as "Panzerkampfwagen I".

The development of the larger tank, the "Grosstraktor", suffered under similar conditions. On March 26, 1927, Rheinmetall, Krupp and Daimler-Benz had been asked to build a full-tracked, armored, amphibious fighting vehicle with a weight not to exceed 20 tons. Each company had built two prototypes by summer of 1928. Anticipated armament was a 7.5 cm Kwk L/20 gun, together with one MG in a fully-rotating turret. As a unique feature, these units had another turret mounted on the rear deck plate, equipped with one MG. Another MG was added during production in the bow of the vehicle. Little is known about the Krupp version of this tank. Rheinmetall started development of their design in 1926 and fitted their units with Cletrac steering. A 250 HP engine allowed the 19 ton unit a top speed of 40 km an hour. The crew consisted of six men. Armor plate was supposed to be 13 mm; actually, all of these "tractors" were made of soft steel. The Daimler-Benz version was designed under the supervision of Prof. F. Porsche. While components were built at the different factories, assembly took place at the Rheinmetall plant in Unterlüss, a little known place where security could easily be maintained. Daimler-Benz used a former aircraft engine of 300 HP to propel their vehicle. The amphibious feature of these vehicles was soon dropped, and the units served mainly, concealed as agricultural tractors, as testbeds for suspension components. It was soon obvious that new ways had to be found to pursue Guderian's basic concept of armored warfare. During this time, the foundation was laid for advanced armored fighting vehicles, which later became the "Panzerkampfwagen III and IV".

In examining foreign developments, the Germans took notice of vehicles such as the British "Independent" and the Russian T-28 and T-35. These were multi-turreted vehicles which emphasized the component firepower to its extreme. In order to investigate this approach, Waffenamt ordered Rheinmetall, in 1933, to develop similar vehicles. They were restricted to a total weight of 24 ton because of the bridge limitations within Germany. In conjunction with Krupp, Rheinmetall built a total of five of these units and called them "Neubaufahrzeug". Wilson and Cletrac steerings were tried, and three of the vehicles were actually built in armor plate of up to 20 mm thickness. These units received the Krupp turret, which mounted a 7. 5 cm tank gun L/23, 5, and a parallel mounted 3.7 cm gun L/45. In addition, one MG was installed in a ball mount at the front plate of the turret. On the right front and left rear top plate of the superstructure, one each MG turret was fitted, mounting two MG 13 each. These turrets were very similar to the production turrets of the Panzer I. It took a six-man crew to man all the weapons. A Maybach engine developing 280 HP gave the vehicle a top speed of 30 km an hour.

The remaining two units were completed in soft steel and fitted with a Rheinmetall turret, having the 37 mm gun installed above the 7.5 cm weapon. They were tested extensively and remained in Putlos for training until the end of the war. The three Krupp turreted units saw action in Norway in 1940, where they disappeared rather rapidly, since maintenance and spare parts supply created too much of a problem.

Rheinmetall built this "Neubaufahrzeug" NbFg. for the Waffenamt.

The Krupp Neubaufahrzeug.

Panzerkampfwagen

The years immediately following the conclusion of World War I were times of much concern as to the development of tanks and tank tactics in Germany. It was a slow and agonizing process in evolution for those directly involved. Much controversy raged among the military men of the world dealing with the employment of the tank in future battles. One side contended that the tank should only be used in support of the infantry, since the tank had been effective when used in this role during the First World War. On the other side, a group of farsighted men such as General Chaffee in the United States of America; General Fuller and Captain Hart of England; Colonel DeGaulle in France; and Major (later Colonel-General) Heinz Guderian of Germany, advocated that the tank, operated en masse as an independent service arm, would produce decisive results, with all other weapons of a formation subordinated to, and in support of, the armor.

Major Heinz Guderian.

Colonel J.F.C. Fuller.

Captain B.H. Lidell-Hart.

The A7V Prototype (wooden body) during testing before Kaiser Wilhelm II and high ranking officers at the Daimler Proving Ground, Berlin-Marienfelde, 19. June 1917.

German A7V Tank 563 "Wotan" Abteilung 1, June 1918 after the action at Villers-Bretonneux, France.

Designed as a replacement for the A7V, Leichter Kampfwagen II could cross a 2m wide trench and carried a 5,7 cm gun.

Apart from the controversy of employment of the tank, Germany was, by the terms of the 1919 Treaty of Versailles, forbidden to develop or purchase armored vehicles although they were allowed to keep some obsolete armored troop-carrying vehicles. This produced many problems for the pro-tank men in their development of the German Tank Force by the complete absence of the item they were striving to develop!

It is natural that new ideas and revolutionary theories are greeted with skepticism by those in responsible positions. It was a long and arduous struggle for Guderian and other tank men in the German Army, to convince the other service arms (steeped in tradition and regarding themselves as "THE" important element) and the Commander-in-Chief of the Army, that their ideas were correct. Guderian's contemporaries also strived, in their respective countries, for the adoption of this theory. He was, however, the first to overcome the many seemingly insurmountable obstacles, and shaped the nature of things as they were to be, which made the German Panzerwaffe the fearsome weapon it was during the Second World War. Progress towards this goal was slow until 1933, when Adolf Hitler became Chancellor. Hitler took a personal interest in armor and motorization, becoming more and more directly involved as the war progressed.

With his theories accepted by the OKW (German High Command), grudgingly by some members, they were effectively and devastatingly proved by the Panzer Divisions at the beginning of World War II. This force commanded by men such as Guderian, Rommel and Hoth, employing fast and hard hitting Panzer units, won for Germany a lightening-like victory against France.

France was an opponent superior in size, armament, and quality of equipment, but lacking in tactics to fully exploit the advantage of their superiority. It should be pointed out, however, there were occasions when French tanks were handled in a proper manner, and in these instances the Germans were hard pressed for their victory.

All work on tanks was not completely halted in Germany after the treaty was signed. A limited amount of development was carried out, but to camouflage this fact it was done under code names. Thus you will find in the pages of history such names as Landwirtschaftlicher Schlepper (LaS) or "Agricultural Tractor," Leicht Traktor or "Light Tractor", and Grosstraktor or "Heavy Tractor". In 1926 the well known German steel complex of Krupp, in cooperation with several other German steel concerns, created the so called "Leicht Traktor", which bore strong resemblances in size and shape to the German light tank of World War I, the LK I and LK II. Further design inspiration was due to the appearance of heavier tanks, up to 70 tons, with stronger armament in France and England. Two examples were the French Char 2C and the English A. 1E. "Independent". Germany also undertook development of a heavier vehicle, the result being the Grosstraktor of 1928.

Landwirtschaftlicher Schlepper (LaS).

13

Although there was limited development of tanks in Germany after the First World War, the interval from that period until 1933, when all restrictions were disregarded, caused a technological lag on the part of industry, since they were not allowed to produce war materials in quantity. Neither the skilled labor, nor the machinery necessary, was available in sufficient quantity to allow a rapid growth of the tank force. The year 1933 is a significant date in the story of German tank development - it marks the beginning of German competition in the armored field. Beginning with the ordering of a design for a light tank in the 5 ton class by the HEERESWAFFE-NAMT (Army Ordnance) and stretching to 1945, by which time the weight of combat tanks had risen sharply, the crowning example - the famous 70 ton Pz. Kpfw. VI Tiger II "Königstiger" armed with the well known 8.8 cm KwK. The "Königstiger", though the heaviest combat tank to participate in World War Two, was dwarfed by the superheavy Pz. Kpfw. "Maus" (Mouse) of 1944/45, a prototype weighing 188 ton, combat loaded. The "Maus" marked the limit in tank development and made it clear that there is a limit to the size and weight in the design of tanks. It amounted to nothing more than an interesting monster of no operational value.

The Krupp Neubaufahrzeug during the occupation of Norway, 1940.

Neubaufahrzeuge

The Krupp Neubaufahrzeug during the Internationale Autoschau, Berlin, February 1937

Seen in the dockyards of Oslo, the Neubaufahrzeug carried a 7,5 cm Kanone with coaxial 3,7 cm Kanone, plus a MG 34 in a Kugelblende. The Pz.Kpfw. type turret to the right of the driver's position holds an additional MG 34 machine gun. The 19,5 t Panzer was crewed by 6 men.

16

Neubaufahrzeug

Panzerkampfwagen I (Sd. Kfz.101)

Original planning for the equipment make-up of the future German Panzer Divisions had called for two types of tanks, one light and one medium. Before these tanks could be built and brought to operational readiness, the planners realized that a considerable amount of time would necessarily pass. What was needed was a tank that would be easier and quicker to produce, until such time as the desired tanks could take their place in the armor formations.

A number of German firms built prototypes, the design of which was based on the Krupp L.K.A. I. Initial production began under the code "LaS," as explained previously. The finished tanks were delivered under the official designation Pz. Kpfw. MG. (Sd. Kfz. 101) Version A. This model was shortly followed by the greatly improved version B. The B had been lengthened to accommodate a new power plant and a fifth road wheel was installed to compensate for the increase. Both models were armed with 2 MG each. Their first taste of battle came during the Spanish Civil War. A number of these remained behind and were incorporated into the Spanish National Army. This conflict pointed out several shortcomings of the Panzer I, but it remained in front line service with the Wehrmacht until after the outbreak of the Second World War.

Some 1,500 of these tanks had been built by 1939 and production did not completely cease until 1941. The campaigns in Poland and France had shown that the Pz. I could not hold pace as an operational weapon and it was relegated to service in tank schools, and as infantry-escort tanks. A new lease on life was given to some, however, due to various conversions, 358 being converted into self-propelled guns,

the Panzer Jäger I, equipped with Czechoslovakian 4.7 cm guns. A commander's tank version was also evolved from the Panzer I, known as the "Befehls-Panzer". It was equipped with powerful radio gear enabling direct command to be exercised over a large and widely scattered armor force. This command was in fact the secret behind operations of large tank forces, and to a large extent, explains how and why the Germans were able to achieve their victories.

One of the highlights of the Reichsparteitag (Reichs Party Day) of 1935 in Nürnberg was the first public appearance of the Panzerkampfwagen I.

Reichsparteitage 1935 in Nürnberg. Panzerkampfwagen I, Ausf. A are lined up on the main approach to the Zeppelinfeld, while a detachment of the Reichsarbeitsdienst (German worker's service) is marching past.

The turret is offset to the right, allowing a driver's access hatch. The rear deck housed a Krupp M305 4 cylinder gasoline engine of 57 horsepower.
Armament consisted of 2 X 7,92mm Dreyse MG 13 machine guns with 1,525 rds. of ammunition. The two man crew consisted of the commander and driver, protected by 13 mm armor plates.

Panzerkampfwagen I (MG) Ausführung A (Sd.Kfz. 101) during training. The girder support is similar to a Carden-Lloyd design, holding the leaf springs of the rearmost road wheel.
Pre-war exercises near Bückeburg, Germany 1933. A fording depth of 60 cm could be achieved.

Reichsparteitag parade ground, Nürnberg 1936. Panzerkampfwagen I Ausf. A was the first mass-produced Panzerwagen by Germany. By the same year, 22 companies of eight machines each had been formed.

Like the Fahrersehklappe (driver's vision ports) seen open here, the turret viewing ports are likewise hinged on internally mounted arms. The commander bears the Iron Cross First Class and Assault Badge.

Once inside the vehicle, the two-man crew of commander and driver communicated by voice tube.

The turret of this Pz.Kpfw. I Ausf. A carries the tactical symbol indicating a headquarters vehicle. Note the leather pads on the underside of the commander's hatch. Cross-country range from the 144-liter tank was 100 km.

This Pz.Kpfw. I Ausf. A of Panzer Abteilung zur besonderen Verwendung 40 (Pz.Abt. z.b.V. 40) provides infantry support with its pair of MG 13 (Dreyse) machine guns. This battalion had 3 companies in Norway, while a fourth was sent to Denmark.

The independent tank battalion Pz.Abt. zbV 40 featured unique insignia: a "V" enclosed in a circle. The company number "3", appears in yellow. Henschel and Maschinenfabrik Augsburg-Nürnberg (MAN) built a total of 477 of these vehicles. Norway, 1940.

With the Zahnradfabrik Friedrichshafen (ZF) Aphon FG31 transmission and increase of 43 hp over the Pz.Kpfw. I Ausf. A, the Pz.Kpfw. I Ausf. B could climb a 30° slope.

The rear deck of the Ausführung B was redesigned with louvers providing supply and exhaust air for the water-cooled engine and its radiator. The five smoke candles could be activated from inside by pull-chains.

Ardennes forest, May 1940. A Panzerkampfwagen I Ausf. B is guided through obstacles made by the Belgians. Two thousand Pz.Kpfw. I Ausf. B were produced, nearly four times the amount of Pz.Kpfw. I Ausf. A. These numbers helped extend their lifespan after obsolescence as munitions carriers and other versions.

Led by the commander's Kleiner Panzerbefehlswagen IB (Sd.Kfz. 265), these Pz.Kpfw. II wait to advance. This vehicle remained in use, both as a commander's vehicle and for artillery observation, long after the original tank version had been withdrawn from combat service.

24

Panzerkampfwagen (MG) Ausf. A (Sd.Kfz. 101)

This Pz.Kpfw. I Ausf. B was captured in Libya and evaluated at Aberdeen Proving Ground Foreign Material Test center in Maryland, USA. The MG 34 weapons replaced the two MG 13 (Dreyse) machine guns. A total of 2,250 rounds of ammunition were carried. It carried a larger engine than the Pz.Kpfw. I Ausf. A, making it necessary to lengthen the hull. This increased the weight by 600 kilograms. An additional road wheel was also added.

Pz.Kpfw. I Ausf. B with rhomboid shaped identification plates. These were featured on vehicles of the early campaigns and resembled the painted shape of later Panzer Division insignia. Warsaw, 1939.

Pz.Kpfw. I Ausf. B could achieve 40 km/h on level roads through five forward speeds. This example leaves a Tankstelle (gas station). The 146 liter tank allowed a road range of 140 km and a cross-country range of 115 km.

26

The commander's split hatch has a smaller door to fire signal flares. The radio aerial could be lowered into the protective trough along the right of the vehicle. It was insulated at the mount by porcelain.

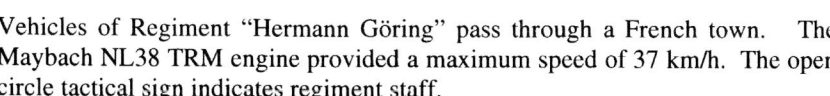

Vehicles of Regiment "Hermann Göring" pass through a French town. The Maybach NL38 TRM engine provided a maximum speed of 37 km/h. The open circle tactical sign indicates regiment staff.

Kl.Pz.Bef.Wg. IB carried Funkgeräte (radios) FuG 6 ultra short wave receiver and FuG 2. The alternator capacity was increased over Pz.Kpfw. IB to charge the wireless batteries. The radio aerial could be lowered into the protective trough along the right of the vehicle.

The crew of 3 shared space with radios, a map table, and a MG 34 machine gun. An extra 15mm of armor was added to the front after experience in Poland.

Designed for infantry support, the Vollkettenfahrzeug (fully-tracked vehicle) VK 1801 was also known as Pz.Kpfw. I Ausf. F. The first two digits "18" designate weight class in tons. The second two are the version of that design.

The VK 1801 featured Schachtellaufwerk (interleaved suspension) with torsion bar suspension. Thickness of hull rear was 50 mm.

This VK 1801 was evaluated at Aberdeen Proving Ground (APG). The weaker sheet metal components are damaged but the thick hull and turret, featuring 80mm of plate at the hull front, remain solid. Krauss-Maffei designed the chassis while Daimler-Benz the superstructure and turret.

Only forty of the Kraus-Maffei Pz.Kpfw. I Ausf.C (VK 601) were produced. They were designed to be light enough to be deployed by aircraft, yet have the necessary speed and armor for reconnaissance. Armor was 30 mm at front and 20 mm at sides, and overall weight was 8,000 kg. This example was captured in Normandy, 1944.

The spoked wheel design saved weight. The outer overlapping wheels have been removed, exposing the axles. Powered by a Maybach HL 45P 6-cylinder engine of 150 hp, a speed of 65 km/h could be achieved. Eight forward and two reverse speeds were available. Sadly, this example at APG was scrapped during the Korean War.

Daimler Benz was contracted to design the superstructure and turret. A triangular bar along the top super-structure front protected the turret ring. Access for the crew of two was restricted to the turret hatch, which had a smaller opening for signal use. Note the triple 90 mm NbK smoke launchers.

The turret had no vision ports; the commander used the eight periscopes of his cupola. Besides his front visor, the driver had one other vision port to his left. Fan-pattern outer wheels distributed weight evenly on the cross-section width, requiring less material.

The turret of this Pz.Kpfw. I Ausf. B has been removed, making the vehicle useful for ammunition resupply. As combat effectiveness declined, many of the turrets of the lighter German tanks were used as armament in fortifications.

Poland, September 1939. A cam acting on the turret ring automatically lowered the antenna when the turret was traversed to the right. A captured helmet is stored near the insulated base socket of the antenna.

Rear hull differences between Pz.Kpfw. I Ausf. A in back and Pz.Kpfw. I Ausf. B in the foreground. The Ausführung B carried a single muffler, and louvers eliminated the rear vision port the driver employed on the Ausführung A.

A restored Pz.Kpfw. I Ausf. A (Sd.Kfz.101) resides at the Deutsches Panzermuseum Munster. The weapons could be fired independently.

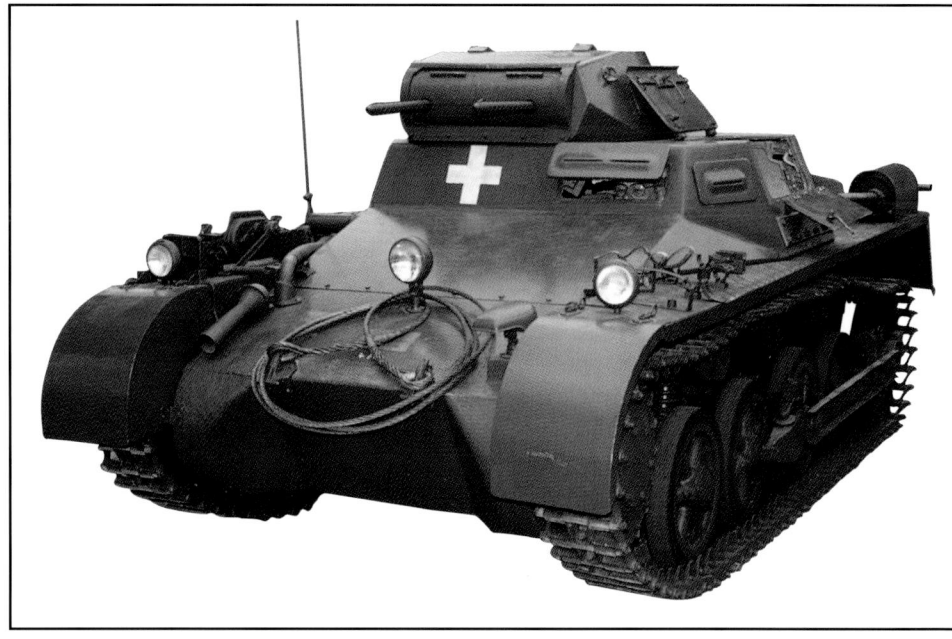

Paint scheme depicts a vehicle from the invasion of Poland. It was found buried in the ground in Southern Germany in 1984 and subsequently restored. A veteran driver of the vehicle, Kurt Fischer, is seen inside.

The idler and rear bogie wheel are paired to articulate on a stub axle. The two center bogie wheels are paired also. The first road wheel has an independent coil spring and hydraulic shock absorber.

Panzerkampfwagen (MG) Ausf. B (Sd.Kfz. 101)

Panzerkampfwagen II (Sd. Kfz. 121)

Designated L.K.A. II (Leichte Kampfwagen Ausland), the firm of Krupp developed this prototype for the lucrative pre-war export market.

In the beginning of 1934 it became clear that production difficulties of the main types of tanks ordered, the later Pz. Kpfw. III and IV, were such that they would not be ready at the time designated for them to enter service. An immediate solution was needed; consequently, orders were placed for the design of a second stop gap tank, which became the Panzer II.

Again a Krupp design, the L.KA II, served as the prototype. In fact the L.K.A. II was a slightly enlarged Pz. Kpfw. I, but lent itself more readily to production than did any of the other designs. Prototypes were begun using the code name, "LaS 100." The Pz. Kpfw. II (2cm) (Sd. Kfz. 121), as the production models were known, was begun in 1935. Minor modifications to the power plants and cooling systems were made in the A and B models. Final form for the Pz. Kpfw. II came with the C model, which had five road wheels instead of the original six. Minor modifications were made to the remaining production models, the F, G, and J, to improve the performance and armor. The D and E models were special versions of the Pz. Kpfw. II. They featured a Christie suspension with four large wheels, similar to the suspension found on the Panther and Tiger Panzer. Two hundred and fifty of these "Schnellkampfwagen", or Fast Armored Vehicles were manufactured and they operated in support of the light cavalry divisions. Armament for all remained the same, one 2cm KwK and one MG.

La.S. 100 (MAN) 'Landwirtschaftliche Schlepper' (agricultural tractor). The name was intended to conceal its true purpose. Five were produced and tested in the summer of 1933 at Kummersdorf testing grounds.

Vehicle of 12. Panzer Division. The 'A96' means Aufklärungs-Abteilung (reconnaissance battalion), 9. Zug (platoon), 6. vehicle. These units carried extra supplies to operate independently for some time.

The division symbol of 4. Panzer Division changed in each of the years 1939, 1940, and 1941, but the 'man-rune' enclosed within a circle dates the image to the campaign for France, 1940.

Panzerkampfwagen II (2cm) Ausf. b (Sd.Kfz.121) was the second model in the development series of the Pz.Kpfw. II, but less than 30 were produced from February to March of 1937.

A Pz.Kpfw. II leads a column during the campaign for Poland. It features the earlier rounded front hull and carries a 2cm KwK 30 (Kampfwagenkanone) and MG 34 in the turret. A total of 180 rounds were carried for the main weapon and 1,425 rounds for the machine gun.

Pz.Kpfw. II Ausf. A of 7. Pz. Div. has additional armor plate bolted to the front of the turret and hull. The 9.5t vehicle could travel at a top speed of 40 km/h and had a range of 170 kilometers.

Several experimental developments were carried out on the Pz. Kpfw. II, one leading to the version L, (Sd. Kfz. 123). Since this vehicle was to be used solely by reconnaissance units, the designation was changed to "Panzer-Spähwagen II" (2cm-KwK. 38) (Sd. Kfz. 123) "Luchs" or Lynx. Some 800 such vehicles were immediately ordered, the last thirty-one being armed with the 5cm KwK L/60 instead of the 2cm weapon, as in the other versions. Production of this model concluded in 1943.

Other developments of the Pz. Kpfw. II led to some D and E models being equipped with flame-throwers, (Sd. Kfz. 122), not many of which were built and these were only used by special units of the Wehrmacht. Experiments were carried out on the Panzer II to waterproof it for use in the proposed invasion of England, "Operation See Löwe" (Operation Sea Lion). Although this operation was cancelled, the experiments later proved their worth during the opening phases in the campaign against Soviet Russia, "OPERATION BARBAROSSA".

The Panzerkampfwagen II cannot be considered superior to any of the opposing Allied tanks at the beginning of the Second World War, though it did form the bulk of the German armored force of the period. The tactics proved to be the superior factor. However, these models were rendered obsolete by 1942, though many continued on in the capacity of self-propelled guns.

Seen in the suburbs of Warsaw on the morning of September 9, 1939, these Pz.Kpfw. II of 4. Panzer Division advance with infantry.

This column, led by an early Pz.Kpfw. II Ausf. A or B, await word to advance in Poland. By 1940, 700 of these vehicles had been built by MAN. They formed nearly 40 percent of the composition of the Panzer Divisions.

A Pz.Kpfw. II Ausf. B of 2.Pz.Div. carries tactical markings indicating a tank of the regimental staff, and 'R02' meaning a spare vehicle. The split commander's hatch was an earlier type.

Pz.Kpfw. II Ausf. D and Sonderanhänger 115 transporters towed by Büssing-NAG trucks. The Ausf. D was designed for speed with double-tired road wheels that also returned the track, and it could reach a maximum of 55 km/h.

The hull design was new, and it was the first German tank to use a horizontal torsion bar suspension. One Panzerabteilung was equipped with them in Poland.

42

The earlier rounded hull front of this Pz.Kpfw. II has been reworked into the box shape. Note the profile of the additional turret armor plate. Such modifications could be introduced on the production line or at the factory when returned for repair.

Experience proved the need for thicker armor for the Pz.Kpfw. II. This Ausf. A or B features additional 20mm plate bolted to the front of the turret, superstructure and hull front.

A Pz.Kpfw. II Ausf. B of Pz.Aufkl. Abt 2 (Recon Battalion), 12. Panzer Division. At turret rear and left hull side is "A" and "94" indicating 9. Zug, 4. vehicle of the Aufklärer-Abteilung.

This Panzer II has a reworked front hull and new cupola with eight episcopes. The superstructure could be unbolted and removed. Hinged track covers prevented debris from accumulating.

Bullet splash guards are placed to protect the turret ring. The door in the glacis plate and the turret hatch gave access to the vehicle. The box on the right sponson has a pair of doors that cover the fuel tank filling necks. The compartment was also used for storage. Note the radio aerial depressed into the protective trough.

Sonderanhänger 115 (Sd.Anh.115) carrying a group of Pz.Kpfw. II (2cm) Ausf. D (Sd.Kfz.121). The tank was powered by the HL62TRM engine with a Maybach Variorex VG transmission, providing seven forward speeds and three reverse.

Pz.Kpfw. II of 15. Panzer Division, 8. Kompanie. The driver sat to the left of the hull and the right side was taken by the large ZF SSG 46 transmission. Two small holes above the driver's vision port allowed the use of a binocular periscope when the vision flap was closed in combat.

Pz.Kpfw. II of 13. Pz. Div., Pz.Rgt. 4. The 2cm KwK 30 main weapon was fed from a small 10-round box magazine because the standard 20-round magazine for the 2cm Flak 30 gun was too large for use in the turret. The weapon was recoil operated and fully automatic.

Panzerkampfwagen II, Ausf. E of 15. Leichte Panzer Division. Derna, North Africa, 1942. All Pz.Kpfw. II in this campaign featured slats cut in the engine deck for additional air circulation and increased radiator fan speed for improved water cooling.

This vehicle bears the new symbol of 7. Panzer Division adopted for Operation Barbarossa, an upright 'Y'. At this time the radio was usually one FuG 2 receiver or Fu5 receiver/transmitter for commander's vehicles. As the war progressed, the standard set in the Pz.Kpfw. II became the Fu5, and unit commanders added another Fu2, requiring space for three radio boxes.

Panzerkampfwagen II (2 cm) Ausf. C (Sd.Kfz. 121)

Earlier years at the APG when some vehicles were displayed indoors. The Pz.Kpfw. II
Ausf. F was captured in Libya, and missing the cylindrical flash suppressor at the end of
the 2cm barrel.

48

Panzerkampfwagen II (2 cm) Ausf. F (Sd.Kfz. 121)

Pz.Kpfw. II Ausf. F at APG. The open flap in the middle of the turret mantlet is for the TZF. 4 sight with 2.5x magnification and 25-degree field of view. The sight was used for both guns and range scaled to a maximum of 1,200 meters.

The MG 34 had it's own port and is seen open, permitting it to be fired over open sights.

Panzerkampfwagen II Ausf. F were produced by Fahrzeug und Motorenbau GmbH of Breslau (FAMO). The superstructure front was straight across the width of the hull to simplify production. As a deception, a false aluminum visor was attached right of the driver's visor in all Ausführung F vehicles.

Panzerkampfwagen II (2cm) Ausführungen A, B, and C vehicles featured road wheels that were independently sprung. Cross-country terrain reduced fuel economy by thirty percent.

Tactical marking of a battalion headquarter staff Pz.Kpfw. I Ausf. A. The Balkenkreuz is segmented to appear on both the hull and the radio aerial trough. When viewed perpendicularly they are perceived as one.

Operation Barbarossa, 1941. A Pz.Kpfw. II Ausf. C and Pz.Kpfw. 38(t) Ausf. E/F of 8. Panzer Division, headquarters staff of II battalion, Panzer Regiment 10.

A Pz.Kpfw. II Ausf. C is preserved at the Musée des Blindés at Saumur, France in colors representative of the early German campaigns.

The Deutsches Panzermuseum Munster restored to running condition the Pz.Kpfw. II Ausf. F that had been at the APG currently at the Wheatcroft Collection in England.

One FuG 12 was carried for longer-range communication and a FuG.Spr.a for contact with other units within short range. The star mast antenna extended the range of the FuG 12.

The vehicles were issued to Panzer Aufklärungs-Abteilungen (reconnaissance battalions) on east and west fronts. It was popular despite 30mm frontal armor and modest 2cm KwK 38 L/55 armament.

Panzerkampfwagen II Ausf. L (Sd.Kfz. 123) "Luchs". The perpetual need for reconnaissance carried Pz.Kpfw. II development further to the Ausführung L. Interleaved suspension and Maybach HL66P engine propelled it up to 60 km/h on roads.

An example of Panzerkampfwagen II Ausf. L still exists today at the Musée des Blindés.

It has even been restored to running condition and often participates in the annual review.

Panzerkampfwagen II Ausf. L "Luchs" (Sd.Kfz. 123)

Pz.Kpfw.II Ausf. L at the APG. It retains original camouflage but the storage box from the right side has been repositioned behind the existing box. Despite a hard fought capture in the Normandy battles, this vehicle was scrapped for the Korean War effort.

55

Panzerkampfwagen II Ausf. L "Luchs" (Sd.Kfz. 123)

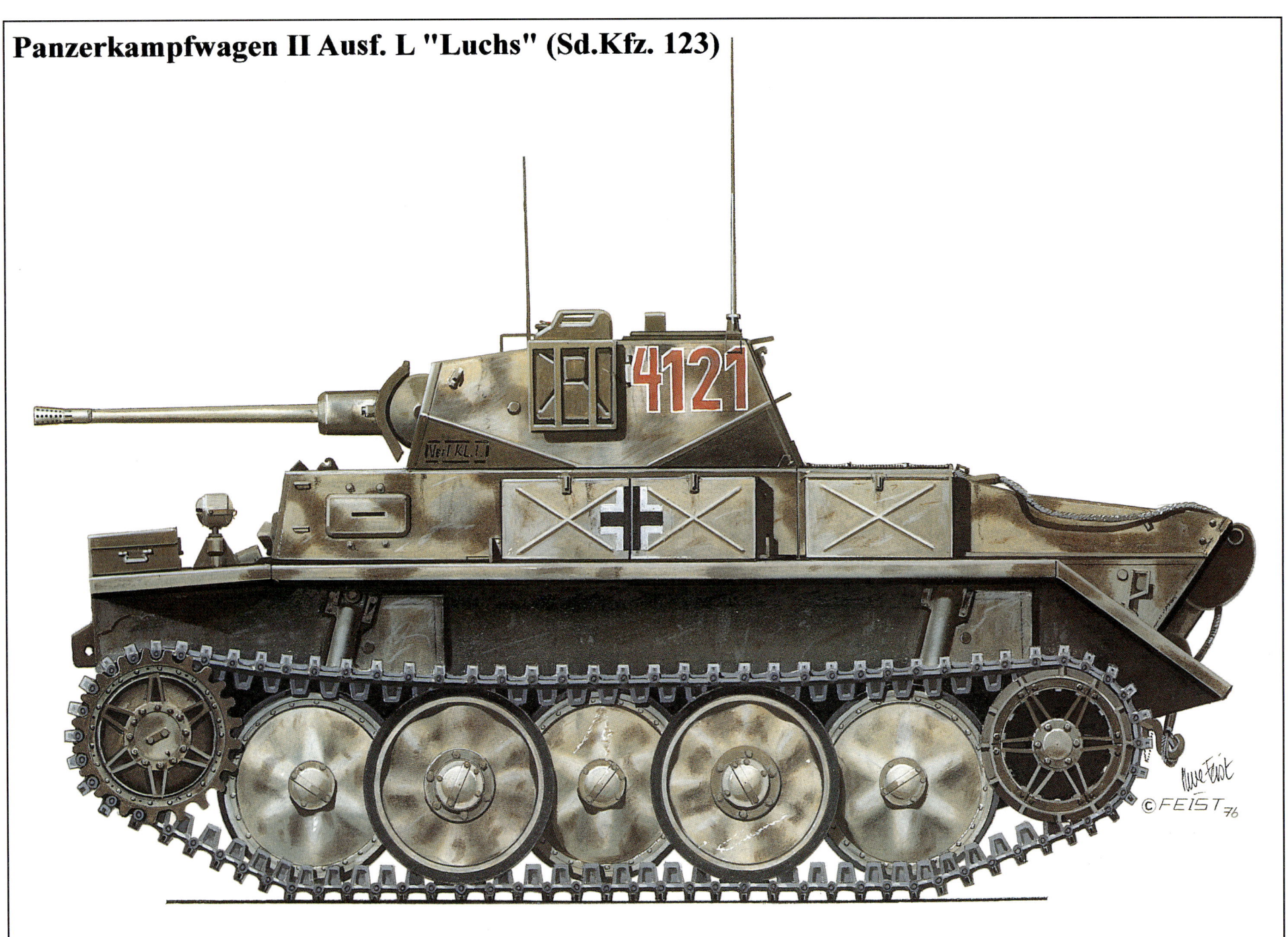

Panzerkampfwagen 35(t) and 38(t)

When the Wehrmacht entered Czechoslavakia in 1938 and took over the Czech Army arsenals, they found two excellent tanks in production. These tanks possessed outstanding qualities; for this reason production was allowed to continue and they were introduced into regular service with the German Army as the Pz. Kpfw. 35(t) and Pz. Kpfw. 38(t).

During the campaign in France the majority of vehicles of the 6th, 7th and 8th Panzer Divisions were Czech. In 1940/41 the Pz. Kpfw. 38(t) formed one-quarter of the total German tank force. This serves to illustrate the importance of these two tanks.

Both vehicles were armed with a 3.7cm KwK cannon and two MG's. This arrangement had been suitable for the battles in France but when operations began in Russia, they proved to be no match for the Soviet tanks. An attempt by Krupp to upgun the 38(t) by the installation of a Pz. Kpfw. IV turret did not prove out and the project was dropped. The 38(t) being of robust and reliable construction was like other German tanks, used for conversions and so continued its service with the Army till the end of the war.

Skoda tanks were also supplied to German allied countries such as Romania and Hungary.

Panzerkampfwagen 35(t) (t="Tschechisch", Czech) was adopted by the Wehrmacht from the Czech Army in 1939.

The Czech LT vz.38 was also brought into German service and redesignated Pz.Kpfw. 38(t). Several adaptations were made, and this vehicle features the German Sehklappe 50 (Observation Port) for both the driver and radio operator and Nova-Technik (NOTEK) light.

Of the 424 Pz.Kpfw. 35(t) produced by Skoda and CKD (Ceskomoravska Kolben Danek), roughly half where in operating condition when employed in the early campaigns. Nevertheless, they filled a substantial inventory gap and proved themselves in combat.

Pz.Kpfw. 35(t) of 6. Panzer Division, first winter in Russia, 1941. The rhomboid-shaped plate was identical to the tactical sign for Panzer units.

Steering system, brakes, and clutch of the Pz.Kpfw. 35(t) were operated by compressed air and were unreliable in the winter season.

Panzerkampfwagen 35 (t)

The turret and hull machine guns have been removed from this vehicle at Aberdeen Proving Ground. All systems were tested and evaluated, even though the long obsolete vehicle was found near the end of the war at Hillersleben, Germany.

Pz.Kpfw. 35(t) was cramped, as the Germans added a fourth crew as loader. The commander also doubled as gunner.

November 1942, near Stalingrad. A Romanian Skoda 126 R-2 of the 1st Royal Tank Division. Identical to Pz.Kpfw. 35(t), differing in name only.

Panzerkampfwagen 35(t)

The 3,7cm Kampfwagenkanone 34(t) L/40 could penetrate 31mm of armor plate at 500 meters and 0° obliquity. A Russian T-28 multi-turreted tank is passed.

The 11. Panzer Regiment of 6. Pz. Div. had seventeen Pz.Kpfw.35(t); three platoons of five each with two retained as headquarters vehicles.

Pz.Kpfw. 35(t) remained in German service for more than three years. As seen here in July of 1941, they were used primarily on the northern sector of the Eastern Front in Russia with 6. Panzer Division.

Riveted construction on the Pz.Kpfw. 35(t) proved to be a weakness, as the force of impacting rounds sent rivet heads flying within the turret.

The majority of the Pz.Kpfw. 35(t) were assigned to 6. Panzer Division. They were powered by a Skoda T11/0 4-cylinder gasoline engine of 115 horsepower. A speed of 34 km/h could be achieved.

The construction of the Pz.Kpfw. 35(t) was sturdy and driven confidently through obstacles. It consisted of flat rolled armor, except for the curved turret plates, all bolted and riveted to an angle iron frame.

64

Pz.Kpfw. 38(t) Ausf. B during the campaign for France. The driver could operate the hull machine gun with a Bowden cable running to the trigger. The weapon had to be locked in place and was aimed by moving the vehicle. The turret machine gun could be aimed independently of the main gun.

The commander rests his hand on his monocular 2.6x periscope, which is tall enough to clear the cupola. This 7. Panzer Division vehicle of Panzergruppe Hoth carries a log for underditching.

Pz.Kpfw. 38(t) of 4.Pz.Div. during maintenance. Access to the Praga EPA 6-cylinder water-cooled gasoline engine was excellent. The two compartment covers opened toward the center as seen here.

Pz.Kpfw. 38(t) with ammunition on a Dniepr River ferry, 1941. Eighteen cases of 300 rounds each were carried internally for the machine guns, and 15 boxes of 3,7cm rounds with 6 shells each.

The hull machine gun has been removed for the additional radio equipment of this command vehicle. The main weapon Skoda 3,7cm UV vz.38 had a very high rate of fire of 15 rounds per minute. This could be achieved because of the semi-automatic breech. The barrel was likely damaged due to natural wear.

The commander's cupola was located off center to the left with one episcope per side. The front one was slightly larger. Basic rear turret and hull thickness was 15mm. Beginning with this Ausführung E, rear turret thickness was increased to 22mm.

This Pz.Kpfw. 38(t) is leaving a specially designed railcar. One such tank carrier car was placed at either end of a BP 42/44 armored train. The hull machine gun was typically removed and the port plated over for this deployment.

A Pz.Kpfw. 38 (t) of 8.Pz.Div. during the early stage of the campaign in Russia, July 1941. Firing range was 4,000m with high explosive and roughly half that for armor piercing at 2,000 meters. Combat effectiveness for armor piercing was best at less than 500 meters.

Despite the ability to climb a 37° slope, this Pz.Kpfw. 38(t) awaits assistance. After passing over the engine, cooling air was forced out through the opening in the rear top plate.

A Pz.Kpfw. 38(t) of 22.Pz. Div, with vehicle number underlined to designate the second Panzer regiment. A unique frame for storage is applied to the turret rear. Internally, a maximum of 18 boxes of 300 rounds each were carried for the machine guns, along with 15 boxes of 3,7cm rounds with 6 shells each.

Pz.Kpfw. 38(t) of 6. Panzer Division at a captured Russian base camp. Joseph Stalin's 1930s purges of the officer corps had degraded his military severely, as evidenced by the early German advances.

Panzerkampfwagen 38(t) of 20. Pz. Div. of 9. Kompanie, Panzer Regiment 21, Eastern Front 1941.

Panzerkampfwagen 38(t)

Panzerkampfwagen III (Sd. Kfz. 141)

The result of the Heereswaffenamt (Wa Prüf. 6) (Army Ordnance Office) order for a light tank to equip those companies of the Armored Detachments, resulted in the creation of the Pz. Kpfw. III. Production difficulties hampered its early appearance in the armored formation, and later the Pz. Kpfw. IV. This was not the only difficulty encountered during the designing of this tank. Much discussion passed between the Army Weapons Office and the Armored Corps concerning the caliber of the main armament of this vehicle. It was considered that a 3.7cm Kwk gun would suffice, but the tank men proposed a 5cm gun be used. The 3.7cm weapon carried the day, due to the fact that infantry formations had already been issued a 3.7cm anti-tank gun, and it was not considered advantageous to produce more than one type of gun. An agreement between the two groups made allowances for the turret to be designed so that a heavier weapon could be installed later.

Development orders were issued to various manufacturers, under the code name "Zugführerwagen (ZW)" or Troop Leader's Vehicle, and Daimler-Benz was awarded the final development and production order. Model A appeared in 1936, followed by the B and C models on which the number of road wheels was changed, six small wheels instead of the original five large ones; few of these types were built. The Panzerkampfwagen III (3.7cm) (Sd. Kfz. 141) was officially accepted by the German Panzertruppe in September 1939.

Demands for improvements due to combat and operational experiences in the Pz. Kpfw. III, were met by additional models. The following is a brief summary of these improvements and modifications. On special "Order of the Führer", a new version of the H appeared in 1940 with strengthened frontal armor. Hitler had also ordered that the 5cm KwK L/60 be fitted in all Pz. Kpfw. III's. These two examples illustrate

how far his interest extended in the design and development of Germany's tanks. The F was the first to receive the 5cm KwK gun which had originally been sought, it also had a luggage box behind the turret; many F's and G's were fitted with tropical equipment and served with the famous "DAK" Deutsche Afrika Korps.

Hitler's order for the 5cm L/60 for the Pz. Kpfw III's had far reaching results. This order was not obeyed, and the shorter 5cm KwK L/42 had been substituted in its place. When Hitler discovered this disobedience, it served to further stimulate his distrust of the General Staff, which increased and lasted until the end of the war, causing many complications in military operations by field commanders.

Poland, 1939. A Panzerkampfwagen III (3,7cm) Ausf. A of 3. Pz.Div. Five large road wheels with coil springs distinguish this type. Only ten of these vehicles were produced.

The 5cm L/60 was introduced in the Pz. Kpfw. III in 1941, becoming the model J. Models L and M were similar to the J but again had increased armor protection. One hundred M's were converted to Flammpanzer III (flame-throwing tanks). The final production model of the Pz. Kpfw. III, the N, appeared in 1942/43. The chassis was the same as the L but with the turret of the Pz. Kpfw. IV, armed with the short barreled 7.5cm KwK L/24, its special purpose vehicle number or Sonderkraftfahrzeug, Sd. Kfz., was 141/2.

Several models of the Pz. Kpfw III were converted into commander's tanks, again with excellent radio equipment, but in order not to draw attention to it, these were fitted with fake wooden cannons, and therefore, appeared as any other normal tank.

Several Pz. Kpfw. III's and IV's, like the Panzer II, had been modified for the invasion of England. Special installations allowed the tanks to be completely waterproofed and enabled them to drive under water up to a depth of 13 feet. These tanks were used during the beginning of the Russian Campaign in 1941 when they literally crossed under the Bug River.

Production of the Panzer III continued until 1943, by which time they had been outclassed by the introduction of the Russian T 34. The chassis of the III's was used for a basis of assault guns and thus continued in production until the end of the war.

Protected by only 15mm thick armor plate, the Pz.Kpfw. III Ausf. A had to be withdrawn from combat units in February of 1940. Daimler-Benz assembled the vehicles and Rheinmetall-Borsig built the turrets.

Pz.Kpfw. III (Fl) Ausf. M (Sd.Kfz. 141/3). During February to April of 1943, 100 tanks produced by MIAG were converted by Wegmann in Kassel to Flammpanzer III (Fahrgcstcll Nr. 77609-77708).

Panzerkampfwagen III (3,7 cm) Ausf. D (Sd.Kfz. 141)

The pair of turret-mounted MG 34 are staggered one in front of the other. This is so the hanging casing catch bags inside do not interfere with each other. Access hatches in the hull front plate were later deleted. Poland, September 1939.

Pz.Kpfw. III Ausf. D is distinguished from earlier models by inclined leaf-spring assemblies to increase support of the first and last pairs of road wheels.   Only thirty were produced in the first half of 1938. They participated in the 1939 invasion of Poland, as seen here with captured helmets.

The Pz.Kpfw. III Ausf. E received the Maybach HL 120TR engine, larger than the HL 108TR of predecessors. A new gearbox had 4 additional forward gears and 3 additional reverse gears. These early vehicles lacked cooling slats in the upper engine deck. Two circular ports for signal use are in the turret roof. A segmented length of armor on the front upper hull protects the vulnerable turret ring from incoming fire.

Pz.Kpfw. III Ausf. F. Overall armor was increased from 15mm to 30mm beginning with the previous Ausführung E model, adding four tons of weight. In addition to the headlights mounted on the towing brackets, small positioning lights were placed on the fenders. A Bosch horn is next to one such light on the right fender.

Panzerkampfwagen III (3,7 cm) Ausf. A (Sd.Kfz. 141)

This Pz.Kpfw. III (3,7cm) Ausf. F is shown at the factory of Wegmann in Kassel, Germany, June 5. 1940. The Ausführung F model was the first version to receive cast air-intakes in the forward upper hull plate, allowing air circulation for final-drive and brake cooling. This vehicle was equipped with the Maybach Variorex 10 speed transmission with pre-selector.

For self-defense, the Pz.Kpfw. III Ausf. F carried a pair of pistol ports in the rear of the turret. The commander's cupola was integrated completely into the turret construction beginning with the later Ausführung H.

The hull-mounted machine gun housing of the Ausführung E was designated Kugelblende 30, indicating the thickness of the armor of 30mm. An improved Fahrersehklappe 30 (Driver's visor) was also included. Only the upper half was adjustable to expose or cover the opening.

Seen in Greece, a Pz.Kpfw. III (3,7cm) Ausf. E (Sd.Kfz. 141). This vehicle is of the first production batch of ninety-six units. Double doors with vision slots and pistol ports replaced the single flap turret doors.

Pz.Kpfw. III Ausf. E. The main improvement over the Ausführung D was the torsion bar suspension design of Dr. Ferdinand Porsche in place of the earlier leaf-spring type. . The suspension required shock absorbers at the first and last wheel positions to dampen the wheels when climbing obstacles. They also kept the tank from continuously oscillating back and forth after hitting a bump in the ground, as with leaf springs.

Panzerbefehlswagen III, Ausf. H. For use in Africa, a larger radiator and air filter were fitted. Nevertheless, the engine had a lifespan of only two to three thousand kilometers in the desert due to the fine silt and heat. Note the 30mm plate bolted to the front hull and superstructure, and the allied ammunition box on the left fender.

Panzerbefehlswagen III, Ausf. H. This vehicle, possibly of 15. Panzer Division, Panzer Regiment 8, would have been one of Oberstleutnant Hans Cramer's headquarters staff vehicles ("R"). A Panzer Division command pennant is carried.

This earlier version of the Pz.Bef.Wg. III, Ausführung H features a false 3,7cm KwK L/45.

A circular hatch in the turret roof of this Pz.Bef.Wg. III, Ausf. H permitted an observation periscope to be raised. Later versions of the Ausführung H carried a dummy main gun resembling the 5cm KwK L/42.

Panzerbefehlswagen III, Ausf. D1. The Ausführung D1 was the first command version of the Pz.Kpfw.III series, and only 30 were built. A frame aerial above the engine compartment was necessary for operation of the FuG 8 radio. The turret was non-rotating.

On either of the superstructure sides, an additional pistol port and visor were added to the Pz.Bef.Wg. III, Ausf. E.

The turret of the Pz.Bef.Wg. III, Ausf. E is bolted in place and the hull mounted MG 34 removed. This vehicle is with 15. Panzer Division, September 1942 near Bardia.

From Feb.1943 to April of 1944, 262 of the Pz.Beob.Wg. III, Ausf. F. were converted from refurbished Pz.Kpfw. III. They were issued to Hummel and Wespe artillery batteries. The work was completed at the Deutsche Eisenwerke factory.

Panzerbeobachtungswagen III, Ausf. G (Sd.Kfz.143) artillery spotting and observation tank. A Turmbeobachtungsfernrohr 2 (TBF-2) periscope extends from the turret roof. The original mantlet of 35mm is replaced by a thicker piece of 50mm, with a cutout for a MG 34 and a fake 5cm weapon.

Early Pz.Kpfw. III used a Maybach transmission with pre-selector that was complicated to maintain. Beginning with the Ausführung H, a simpler ZF SSG 77 Aphon transmission was substituted.

A newly designed drive sprocket and idler wheel came with the Ausführung H. The first return roller was moved slightly forward. The tracks were also widened to 400mm to distribute the added weight of the new gun and armor. Vehicle of 1. Pz. Div.

Beginning with the Pz.Kpfw. III, Ausf. H, the turret was redesigned to accommodate the larger 5cm KwK 38 L/42. A turret storage basket was also fitted for the first time. The rear turret plate was made of a single piece, eliminating the bulge below the cupola. A 30mm plate was bolted to the hull front in addition to the basic 30mm armor.

Pz.Kpfw. III Ausf. G submersible Panzer. An armored housing can be seen all along the base of the turret ring. This protected a rubber tube that inflated to prevent water entry. The waterproof cover for the engine side air intake is raised.

Because the unit was formed from personnel of Pz.Rgt. 6, 3. Panzer Division, the vehicles carried the standing bear emblem of 3.Pz.Div. as well as 4.Pz.Div. markings.

Pz.Kpfw. III, Ausf. G of 4. Panzer Division. The men are volunteer specialists of Pz.Abt. (T)C, a unit temporarily attached to 4. Pz. Div. They were trained to use the modified seaworthy Panzer in amphibious invasions.

Panzerkampfwagen III (5 cm) Ausf. F (Sd.Kfz. 141)

The emblem of 4. Pz. Div. is readily apparent. Note the wide flange outlining the hull MG port and gun mantlet. These received waterproof fabric covers, sealing the openings from water. The newly introduced 5cm KwK L/42 main weapon is carried.

The submersible tanks were simplified for river crossing after Operation Seelöwe was cancelled. Panzer Regiment 18 used them to cross the River Bug on June 22, 1941 during Operation Barbarossa.

The taller exhaust pipes developed for these vehicles were reintroduced for Pz.Kpfw. III Ausf. M production. Though the exhaust was fitted with non-return valves, a bilge pump extracted any water that made it inside. Prearranged explosive charges could remove the numerous seals once on land. This prevented the engine from overheating.

Pz.Kpfw.III (5cm KwK L/42), Ausf. J (Sd.Kfz. 141). This model represented the most common version of the Pz.Kpfw. III with over 1,500 examples produced to July 1942. The hull was lengthened by an engine deck extension to the rear.

The housings for final drive and brake cooling in the hull front were redesigned to accept the new armor thickness. Air was pulled by the radiator fans through the housings and into tubes leading under the floor to the engine compartment.

Overall armor thickness, including rear plates, was increased to 50mm with the Ausführung J. This change required a new design for the hull machine-gun mount (Kugelblende 50) and driver's visor (Fahrersehklappe 50). Single piece gearbox access hatches in the hull front were also introduced.

89

Pz.Kpfw.III, Ausf. J of 14. Panzer Division. The length of the 5cm KwK 39 L/60 can be appreciated in this view. The TZF5d gunner's periscope had a 2.5 magnification and a 25 degree field of view, which was adjustable in 100 meter increments to a range of 1500 meters for Panzergranate (AP) shells and 3000 meters for Sprengranate (HE) ammunition.

The Sternantenne (Star Antenna) of this Panzerbefehlswagen III Ausf. K increased the range of the FuG 8 radio. It replaced the revealing frame antenna. The Pz.Bef.Wg. III Ausf. K was the first of Pz.Kpfw. III command series to carry a full armament.

Panzerbefehlswagen III with 5cm KwK L/42 (Sd.Kfz.141). The Ostketten (wide ice tracks) were attached to reduce the ground pressure of the vehicle.

A Pz.Kpfw.III Ausf. M leads this column of 6. Pz. Div. vehicles seen during the Kursk offensive. The Sd.Kfz. 250 has the division's Kursk symbol in white. Triple 90mm NbK smoke mortars on either side of the turret replaced the rear mounted smoke candles.

90

Panzerkampfwagen III (5 cm) Ausf. G (Sd.Kfz. 141)

The Deutsches Panzermuseum Munster restored to running condition the Pz.Kpfw.III (5cm), Ausf. M (Sd.Kfz. 141).

Preserved at the Musée des Blindés is this Pz.Kpfw.III Ausf. E. This example has been refitted with the 5cm KwK L/42 in an external mantlet and received 30mm of extra armor plate bolted to the hull front. The conversions took place between August 1940 and 1942. Also added is the spaced armor covering the superstructure front.

Panzerkampfwagen IV (Sd. Kfz. 161)

The Pz. Kpfw. IV (7.5cm) (Sd. Kfz. 161) was the last tank designed during peace time in Germany and filled the design order for a medium tank. During the planning of the medium tank, it was envisioned that the function performed would be dual: first, to support the light tank, and second, armed with a heavier caliber weapon it would engage targets out of range of the light tanks, thus the 7.5cm Kwk gun for the mediums.

The first production vehicle left the assembly lines in 1936. It is interesting to note that the chassis of this first model was, in principle, kept without any essential modifications throughout the whole production cycle of the Pz. Kpfw. IV, which concluded with the end of the war.

All early models, B thru E and F 1, had increased armor protection, and were armed with the short 7.5cm KwK and two MG 34. Krupp had been ordered to develop a new long barrel 7.5cm cannon, which became the 7.5cm KwK 40 L/43. To accommodate this gun, the turret had been redesigned.

Thus it was that the first of the F series that went into production still kept the short 7.5cm gun, while the later ones were fitted with the new long 7.5cm gun and were designated Pz. Kpfw. IV F-2.

As usual, successive models appeared with increased armor and other minor modifications. The H series (Sd. Kfz. 161/2) had 5mm steel plates called "Schürzen" (aprons) suspended from the hull sides to serve as protection to the tank tracks. The J model, and final version of the reliable IV, featured the installation of the "Ostkette" which increased the width of the tank tracks for better operation in the formidable mud and snow of Russia. The 5mm aprons were replaced by woven wire in the same shape as the plate aprons.

German tank production capacity was very weak at the beginning of the Second World War. This is pointed out by the fact that at the commencement of the campaign in the West there were only 278 Pz. Kpfw. IV's available. As time passed, production increased, and despite bombings by the Allies, Germany was able to produce more tanks near the end of the war than she did in the beginning.

Without exaggeration it can be said that the Pz. Kpfw. IV was not the best German armored fighting vehicle, but it was the backbone of the Armored Corps. It performed its duty wherever and whenever called upon. Numerous modifications utilizing the chassis of the IV were made.

The Pz. Kpfw. IV had been designed to meet the standards required for the medium tank component of the new German Panzer Divisions and became the last German tank designed during peace time.

Pz.Kpfw. IV Ausf. H of 3.Pz.Div. in Russia, winter 1943-44. The standing bear division emblem can be seen on the turret armor skirt.

DEVELOPMENT HISTORY

Formulated as early as 1930, the order for the initial prototype vehicles was issued to industry at the beginning of 1934. Concealed under the code name "Bataillonsführerwagen" or "BW", these orders went to the companies of Krupp and Rheinmetall-Borsig. Rheinmetall presented its first prototype in 1934, but it was Krupp, Essen who received the final production order. The suggested solution incorporated features of both vehicles and presented itself as a fully-tracked armored fighting vehicle, carrying a 7.5 cm Kwk tank gun and one MG in a 360° rotating turret. Another MG was provided in the front plate. With a total weight of 18 metric tons, the unit had frontal armor of between 16 to 20 mm strength, while the sides were 13 mm thick. A five-man crew, having each distinct responsibilities, was to man the vehicle. Equipped with a 300 HP Maybach gasoline engine, the unit employed steering clutches and frontal final drives. Krupp manufactured its first production model in 1936 and named it "Panzerkampfwagen IV" Ausf. A. The official Ordnance Dept. designation was "Versuchskraftfahrzeug 622". Thirty-five of these vehicles were built between 1936 and 1937. These units were recognizable by a front plate where the portion on the left-hand side in front of the driver was further forward than the right-hand side portion. A circular ball MG mount for the radio operator and a rectangular side view opening for the driver completed the front plate. Extending from the rear plate of the turret was a prominent, drum-shaped commander cupola with simple, unsophisticated vision slits. These 0-series vehicles served as test beds for the development of further production models.

The rare Pz.Kpfw. IV (7,5cm) Ausf. A (Vs Kfz. 622). Only 35 were produced. Komota, Sudetenland, 9.10.1938. The cupola has eight vision slits and the driver's compartment is further forward to provide him a view to the right.

Panzerwagen IV (7,5 cm) Ausf. C (Sd.Kfz. 161)

Pz.Kpfw. IV (7,5cm) Ausf. C (Sd.Kfz.161) in Poland. Double hinged doors provide access to the brakes in the hull front. The loader's front turret vision port is open. This port was included all the way to Ausführung G production.

Panzerkampfwagen IV (7,5 cm) Ausf. D (Sd.Kfz. 161)

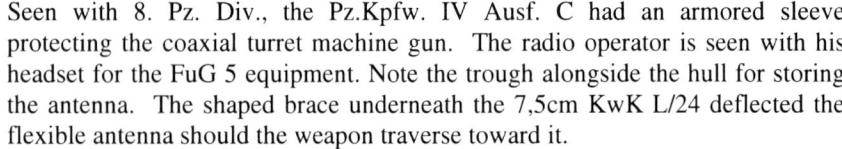

Seen with 8. Pz. Div., the Pz.Kpfw. IV Ausf. C had an armored sleeve protecting the coaxial turret machine gun. The radio operator is seen with his headset for the FuG 5 equipment. Note the trough alongside the hull for storing the antenna. The shaped brace underneath the 7,5cm KwK L/24 deflected the flexible antenna should the weapon traverse toward it.

Pz.Kpfw. IV Ausf. C with 5. Panzer Division; the emblem is weathered. Two-digit numbers were standard for this division, representing platoon and vehicle number. Note the pistol port for the radio operator in the hull front. The conical shaped cover on the turret roof protected the left signal port. It protected signal lamps used by the commander.

For self-defense, a pair of pistol ports was furnished in the rear turret and each turret door. There is also a rack of five smoke candles above the muffler. Protecting the engine intake louver is a length of spare track. Above it is the gun cleaning rod for the 7,5cm KwK L/24. To the left is a track adjustment tool. Pz.Kpfw. IV Ausf. C of 2. Panzer Division.

98

A Pz.Kpfw. IV Ausf. A (at left) and Ausf. C (right) of 3. Panzer Regiment. Note the difference in cupola design and vision ports at turret front. The hull MG 34 was omitted with Ausführung C production but reintroduced quickly with the next model.

Two Pzkpfw. IV Ausf. A in Poland, September 1939. The Balkenkreuz of the leading vehicle has been darkened to reduce contrast. An auxiliary engine powered an electric generator, which, in turn, provided turret traverse for the 7,5cm main weapon.

Nineteen hundred thirty-seven saw the introduction of the second model of the Panzer IV, the Ausführung B. The front plate of the model B extended straight across the tank in one plane. There was a revolver port well over on the right-hand side and a square visor in the position occupied before by the hull machine gun mounting on the Ausführung A. The Maybach "HL 120 TR" engine replaced the former "HL 108" power plant. Forty-two of these vehicles were completed by 1938.

The Ausführung C followed in 1938, being very similar to the former version. A straight frontal plate still being an obvious recognition feature of this vehicle. The turrets of both Ausf. B and C were practically identical, having a modified commander cupola when compared with Model A. Ausf. B, however, had a different type of aerial deflector and was without any armored sleeve protecting the turret machine gun. Starting with serial number 80341 the Maybach "HL 120 TRM" engine was installed. Nineteen hundred thirty-eight also introduced the following version, the Ausführung D. This vehicle, again, had the staggered frontal plate, originally introduced with the model A. A square shaped ball-mounted MG appeared again for the radio operator, while the driver was provided with a side opening for a sub-machine gun. The gun shield for the main armament was now externally mounted. The tracks for both Ausf. D and E had higher guide teeth and could not be used for former versions. In contrast, tracks used on the models A through C could, without difficulties, be utilized for Ausf. D and E.

One hundred and fifty units of the next model were completed by December of 1939. Still showing the staggered frontal plate, both the driver vision slit and the ball mount for the radio operator were modified. An improved commander cupola was installed in a different fashion. It no longer protruded from the rear plate of the turret.

Panzerkampfwagen IV (7,5 cm) Ausf. E (Sd.Kfz. 161)

The Pz.Kpfw. IV Ausf. E featured a redesigned commander's cupola and drive sprocket,
a fume extractor fan on the turret roof, and a new Fahrersehklappe 30 (driver's visor).
The brake access hatches have only one hinge instead of two.

Panzerkampfwagen IV (7,5 cm) Ausf. F-1 (Sd.Kfz. 161)

Production of the Pz.Kpfw. IV Ausf. F began in April 1941. This example displays the new superstructure front with a single 50mm plate. A new machine-gun mounting (Kugelblende 50) and an improved visor for the driver (Fahrersehklappe 50) have also been installed on account of the new thickness.

Pz.Kpfw. IV Ausf. D

The 7,5cm KwK L/24 gun was rifled with 28 grooves and could fire K.Gr.rot Pz. (AP), Gr.34 (HE), and Gr.38 (Shaped charge) rounds. Velocity ranged from 385m/s for AP to 450m/s for the shaped charge. Elevation of the gun was -10 to +20 degrees.

Already in September of 1939, after conclusion of the hostilities in Poland, the Panzer IV was officially declared standard issue of the tank regiments and received the designation "Panzerkampfwagen IV" (Sd. Kfz. 161). Battle experience with these units in both Poland and France soon pointed out the inadequate protection afforded by the frontal armor. Spaced armor plating appeared, therefore, on most of these vehicles, starting in 1940. Production of the Panzer IV was originally limited, since it was supposed to equip only one company out of the four available to a standard tank battalion. Thus, 1939 saw the production of only 45 Panzer IV's, while the total Panzer IV production for 1940 amounted to 280 units. Two hundred and seventy-eight Panzer IV participated in the campaign against France in 1940.

After successfully concluding this battle, several tank formations were ear-marked to participate in the operation "See Löwe" (Sea Lion), the anticipated invasion of England. Panzer IV within these outfits were made submergible by means of simple modifications. They were to be dropped from barges in front of the British coast and were to drive under water until they reached the shore. Tests turned out to be successful but since the invasion itself never materialized, these tanks formed the nucleus of the 18th Armored Division, which forded the river Bug at the beginning of the campaign against Russia in 1941.

Nineteen hundred forty saw a basic change in the Panzer IV production with the appearance of the Ausf. F. The basic armor was now increased from 30 to 50 mm. The frontal plate was straight across the tank again and an improved driver vision visor and radio operator MG mount were installed. The track width was increased from 380 to 400 mm, to compensate for the additional weight. Turret hatch doors were changed to a pattern similar to the one used on the Panzer III, the single door being replaced by two hinged covers. Main armament was still the short-barreled 75 mm gun. Production

The introduction of an externally attached mantlet, along with wider tracks, distinguished the Pz.Kpfw. IV Ausf. D. This example is serving with 6. Panzer Division.

The firms of Nibelungenwerke in Sankt Valentin and VOMAG in Plauen built the Pz.Kpfw. IV Ausf. F. The drive sprocket and rear idler wheel were redesigned. This was also the first model to receive double doors in the sides of the turret.

In a major increase of firepower, the Pz.Kpfw. IV, Ausf. F-2 featured the 7,5cm KwK 40 L/43. The turret area was rearranged to accommodate the larger weapon. Note the single-baffle muzzle brake, superceded by a double-baffle design in subsequent models.

Pz.Kpfw. IV (7,5cm), Ausf. G (Sd.Kfz.161/1). After June of 1942, a plate of 30mm thickness was added to the basic 50mm plate of the superstructure front, along with 90mm NbK smoke dischargers. These vehicles of 1. Panzer Division are deployed in Greece, July 1943.

of this model run continued deep into 1941. Russia was attacked in the meantime and first battle experience revealed a completely new enemy to the German Panzertruppe. New tanks and anti-tank weapons employed by the Russians out-classed almost everything the Germans had. In an emergency measure, all available means were used to stabilize the threatening situation. Many a makeshift solution was accepted and specific orders to the tank building industry asked for larger tank guns. In November of 1941, a long-barreled main armament for the Panzer IV was demanded and installed in Panzer IV vehicles as early as March of 1942. The version thus equipped was called Ausf. F-2, while F models retaining the short weapon received the designation Ausf. F-1. Recognition feature of the F-2 version was the ball-shaped muzzle brake of the gun which was replaced on the following version G with a double baffle muzzle brake typical for most German vehicles of this era.

Ausführung G came off the production lines in 1942 and was manufactured mainly at the Nibelungenwerke of St. Valentin in Austria. The move from the original Krupp-Gruson factory in Magdeburg was motivated mainly by the ever-increasing Allied air raids against German war industries. Both F 2 and G models had the long weapons with a barrel length of L/43. Ausf. G, however, had a side armor of 30 mm compared to the 20 + 20 mm protection of the F series. Its roof armor was increased from 10 to 15 mm. Sometimes additional 30 mm plates were attached to the front sections of the vehicles.

By June of 1942, the industry had received an order to increase the frontal plates of the Panzer IV to 80 mm. At the same time, the final main armament with a length of L/48 was available and was installed in the Ausf. H, the main equipment of Panzer formations during 1943. In order to defeat the effect of the very powerful Russian antitank rifles and for protection against hollow-charge projectiles, side armor plates were attached to most German armored fighting vehicles. These skirts were also applied around the turret, which allowed the omission of the usual turret side vision slots. The hatch cover for the cupola was now a circular, one-piece lid contrary to the double flap used on previous models.

With additional radio equipment, but reduced ammunition stowage, vehicles of the H production run could be used as command vehicles. They Were officially called "Panzerbefehlswagen IV".

During this time, the company Zahnradfabrik Augsburg had developed an experimental hydraulic steering system, new and different from anything the Germans had previously used. Using a Panzer IV Ausf. H. chassis, a Thoma oil drive transmission system was installed. The power train consisted of two wobble plate oil pumps assembled into a single unit and driven by the usual Maybach HL 120 power plant. The driver controlled the vehicle by supplying varying torques for steering and driving. At the same time, a hydraulically-operated turret traversing and gun elevating system was incorporated. These tests were never concluded. For adverse weather conditions in Russia, Panzer IV vehicles received the so-called "Ostkette" a widened track which decreased considerably the ground pressure of the vehicle.

March of 1944 saw the introduction of the final mark of the Panzer IV, the Ausführung J. The two-cycle gasoline engine, used for driving the electric motor for the turret traverse, was now omitted and instead, an additional fuel tank of 200 liter capacity installed. Some of the late production vehicles had a wire mesh side protection instead of the usual skirt armor. Panzer IV of the J version remained in production until April of 1945. Total production of Panzer IV vehicles amounted to approximately 9000 units. Krupp investigated toward the end of the war the feasibility of installing the "Panther" gun in a Panzer IV turret. Wooden mock-up models were prepared, but the chassis proved to be completely overloaded. The project was dropped. Because of raw material shortages, some of the late Panzer IV chassis also came equipped with

only three instead of the customary four return rollers. Panzer IV were also employed in small numbers by various German satellite countries, such as Hungary, Rumania and Bulgaria. Spain and Turkey received a token number of these vehicles.

Seen on this Pz.Kpfw. IV Ausf. H. is an early design pattern for the Panzerschürzen, which were fixed rigidly to a frame. These could limit the vehicle movement when snagged. A new drive sprocket of welded and webbed construction is seen.

Beginning in August of 1942, the 7,5cm KwK 40 L/43 was introduced to Pz.Kpfw. IV Ausf. F production. Its longer barrel and larger ammunition increased the overall weight of the tank (23t vs. 22.3t) and reduced its speed (40km/h vs. 42km/h). The crews, however, welcomed the improved firepower against the Russian T-34.

Panzerkampfwagen IV Ausf. F-2 (Sd.Kfz. 161)

Pz.Kpfw. IV Ausf. G with single baffle muzzle brake. Beginning with Ausf. G production, the loader's vision port at the turret front was omitted. The wheel trough has been relocated in a non-standard position. This vehicle at the APG is a combination put together to attempt a complete vehicle.

Pz.Kpfw. IV Ausf. G of 10. Pz.Div. with an "8" indicating 8. Kompanie, and "23" the 3. Panzer of the 2. Zug, Panzer Regiment 7. At 500 meters using Panzergranate 40 ammunition, 154mm of armor could be penetrated. The round traveled at 930 meters per second.

Vision ports for the loader and gunner in the turret sides were omitted in the Pz.Kpfw. IV Ausf. G. Normally the road wheel box on the left fender carried only two spares but this vehicle in Tunisia has been field modified to fit three.

This late production Pz.Kpfw. IV Ausf. G in Russia has the split cupola hatches, replaced by a single piece beginning with the Ausf. H. A paired wheel assembly from the left side has broken its weld and is stored on the glacis plate. "Ostketten" ice cleats have been installed to reduce ground pressure.

Panzerkampfwagen IV (7,5 cm) Ausf. G   (Sd.Kfz. 161)

Pz.Kpfw. IV Ausf. J newly issued to a Waffen-SS unit, 1945.

Panzerkampfwagen IV (7,5 cm) Ausf. J (Sd.Kfz. 161)

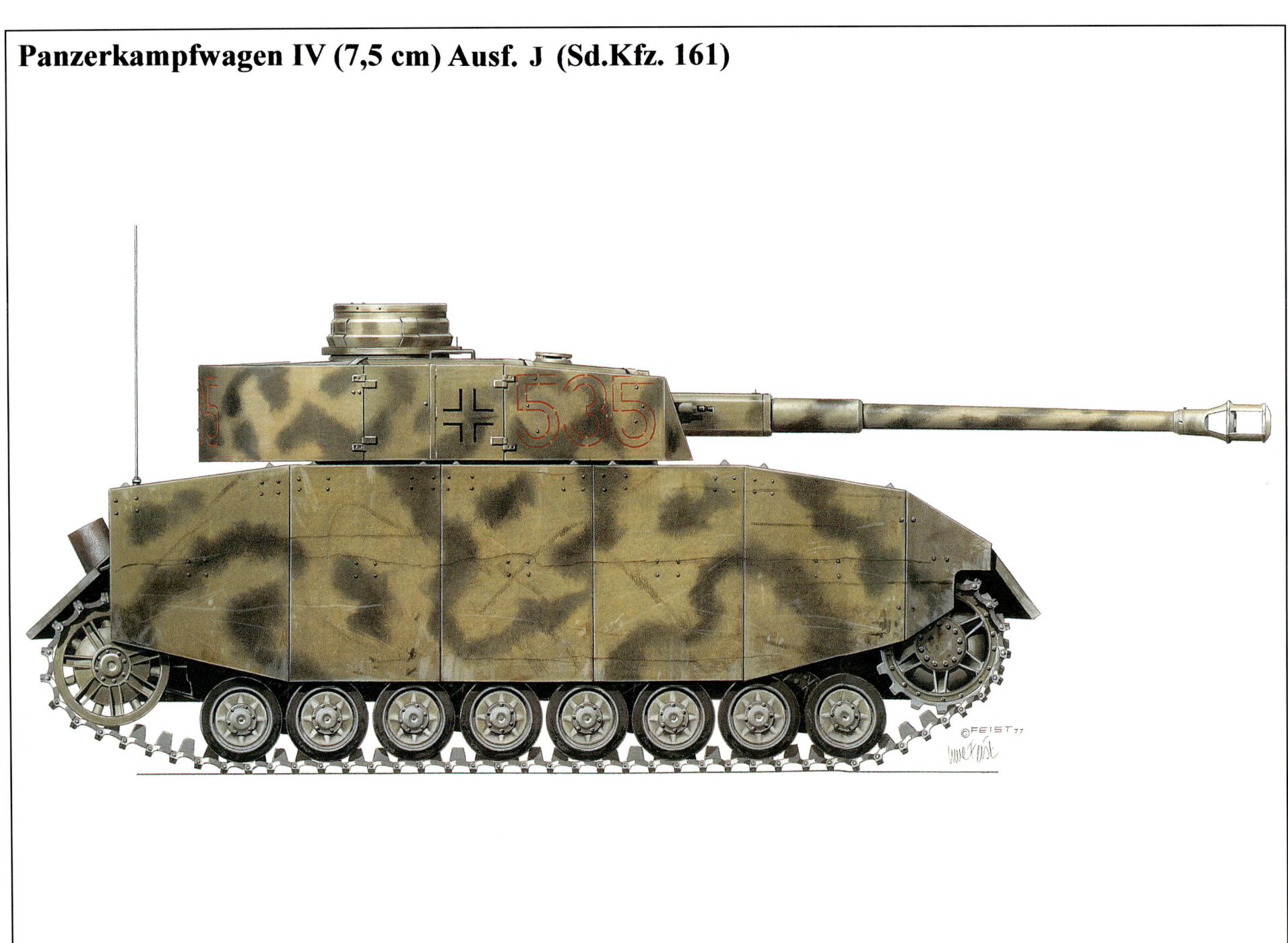

Pzkpfw. IV Ausf. H training in France, early 1944, 2. Panzer Division, Panzer Regiment 3. Single piccc cupola hatches were introduced with the Ausführung H. A speed of 40 km/h could be reached on roads and about half that speed cross-country.

In 1983, the Deutsches Panzermuseum Munster completed restoration of a Pz.Kpfw. IV. Here it is seen on Panzer Testing Ground "Kohlenbissen", 21 August 1993. Manufacture of this Ausführung G, Fahrgestell Nr. 83072 was completed by VOMAG in September 1942.

Features of early Ausführung G production are present. The glacis plate has the brackets for mounting 7 track links, introduced in June 1942. The spare road wheel box on the left fender is a standard type without lock rod. Two holes above the driver's vision port are for the episcope.

The vehicle was shipped to Tobruk and issued to Pz.Rgt. 8 on October 21, 1942. When captured by the British, there were 482 kilometers on the odometer. The turret serial number is 82552, assigned by VOMAG during late Ausführung F1 production. The gun is a 7,5cm KwK 40 L/43.

Zahnradfabrik Augsburg built one prototype with hydrostatischem Antrieb (experimental hydrostatic drive). The example is preserved at the APG and utilized a Pz.Kpfw. IV Ausf. G as a basis. Now driven from the rear, the new equipment permitted more space in the main compartment.

Heavy gauge wire mesh Panzerschürzen replaced the 5mm mild steel plate as a material conservation measure. They were introduced on later production vehicles such as this Pz.Kpfw. IV Ausf. J, seen at Musée des Blindés.

116

Pz. Kpfw. V "Panther" (Sd. Kfz. 171)

The next tank design, after the Pz. Kpfw. IV, would naturally be the Pz. Kpfw. V. In fact two tanks bore this designation, and the older version should not be confused with the Pz. Kpfw. V Panther, a most important tank in German military history. The older version, Nb. Fz., appears to have been inspired by the British "Independent" and the Russian T-28 and T-35. Very little is known about this tank. Approximately six were built. It has been said that they were built for propaganda purposes, but in actual fact, they were used in Norway. Since the Nb. Fz. may be considered only as an experimental vehicle, it became necessary for another Pz. Kpfw. V to be developed.

The Russian T-34 may be considered directly responsible for the development of the Pz. Kpfw. Panther. The T-34 came as a shocking surprise to the German High Command. When encountered, it inflicted serious losses to the Panzer Divisions. Until this time the Germans had enjoyed the advantage of superior tanks, but men like Guderian realized that the T-34 would greatly influence German tank design in the future. General Guderian himself requested that a commission, composed of representatives of the Army Ordnance Office, the various tank designers and firms engaged in tank construction, be sent to the battlefield, and by close examination of knocked out tanks and from first hand reports, determine what was needed to counter this menace. There can be no doubt that their findings dictated the design of the Panther.

Production of the Panther Ausf. D (Sd. Kfz. 171) began in November 1942.

Besides mechanical malfunctions, the Panther D, armed only with the 7.5cm KwK L/70, suffered from lack of self-defense. This was also the case of the Panzer Jäger "Elefant", no bow machine gun. The Panther A followed the D into production, similar in appearance but featuring a bow machine gun for its own protection. Steel aprons similar to those on the Pz. Kpfw. IV H could also be fitted.

The model G followed the A and had a modified hull. A's and G's proved their abilities up to the end of the war and were greeted with success wherever they appeared. It was more than a match for any other Allied tank, including the T-34. The Panther stopped the T-34 menace on the Eastern Front, the Tiger I and II could have eliminated it. They were not out fought, just out produced.

The turret of this Panzerkampfwagen Panther Ausf. D is reversed in preparation for recovery. The tight fit of the Maybach HL230P30 in the engine compartment required adequate cooling to avoid component failure. This and other problems hindered the early production Panthers.

DEVELOPMENT HISTORY

Panzerkampfwagen VK 3002 (MAN) prototype with experimental single baffle muzzle brake. Front drive sprocket design is also unique to this vehicle and was not produced. Interleaved wheels sprung on double torsion bars provided excellent stability.

Russian T-34/42, thoroughly burned out.

Orders to create replacement vehicles for the Panzerkampfwagen IV were placed by the German Ordnance Department, as early as the spring of 1937. They went to the companies of Henschel & Sohn, Daimler-Benz AG., Maschinenfabrik Augsburg-Nürnberg AG., and Dr. Ing. h.c.F. Porsche KG. Specified was a vehicle of the 30 ton class, which was to be equipped with either the 7.5 cm Kwk L/24 or a 10.5 cm Kwk L/28 gun. All companies involved completed their prototype vehicles by 1941 without seeing any chance for a production order, since the Panzer IV proved to be quite successful and adequate armored fighting vehicle.

This situation was changed overnight with the appearance of the Russian T-34, which was encountered by German troops entering Russia for the first time in July of 1941. This vehicle by itself rendered the entire German tank and anti-tank weaponry useless and asked the German High Command for drastic measures to counter-balance the Russian advantage. Immediate suggestions were to copy the main features of the T-34, such as the hull shape, the power to weight ratio and the ground pressure were concerned. All previous German tank designs were frozen. Henschel and Porsche immediately pursued the incorporation of the 8.8 cm gun as main armament in a vehicle of approximately 45 tons, while Daimler-Benz and MAN received an order from the Ordnance Department on November 25, 1941, to create a 30 ton armored vehicle with inclined hull walls, a frontal armor of 60 mm and a high velocity weapon. All designs were completed on paper by April of 1942, and after their final evaluation by the "Panther" committee in May of 1942, the MAN design was chosen for production. The first soft-steel prototype was

118

already completed in September of the same year, while production started in November of 1942. It was to nobody's surprise that the first model, coming off the production line showed serious deficiencies which continuously plagued tank formations receiving these vehicles. With their weight increased to 43 metric tons, these units received the official designation "Panzerkampfwagen Panther", Ausführung D (Sd. Kfz. 171).

The first twenty vehicles were fitted with 60 mm frontal armor, subsequent models had their glacis plates increased to 80 mm. A 700 HP Maybach twelve-cylinder gasoline engine type "HL 230 P 30" drove the front sprockets via a synchronized ZF 7-speed gearbox. A contemplated B version was supposed to be equipped with a Maybach OLVAR pre-selective transmission, used on the "Tiger" vehicles. Obvious recognition features of the first production model were the drum-shaped commander's cupola and the lack of a ball-bearing mount for the MG in the glacis plate. The very first models received a gun with a ball shaped muzzle brake, which was soon replaced by a double baffle brake common on most German tank guns.

Joining MAN in the production of these much-needed vehicles were the Maschinenfabrik Niedersachsen-Hannover as of February, 1943. Henschel & Sohn produced 200 "Panther" units from March through November, 1943, and last but not least, Daimler-Benz, after abandoning their own "Panther" design, contributed substantially to the production of these vehicles.

Nineteen hundred forty-three saw the introduction of the second production model, the Ausführung A. The only outside changes compared to Ausführung D were the installation of a ball-mounted MG in the sloped front plate and a considerably modified commander cupola. Most of the vehicles had received the obligatory skirt armor to protect their exposed flanks. "Zimmerit" anti-magnetic mine paste and an AA MG

Early production model Panther Ausf. D. (Sd.Kfz.171) with pair of headlights, drum-shaped cupola and rectangular MG port. Steering gear and brakes were developed by MAN and operated hydraulically. Each track could be stopped separately. The commander's cupola of the first 30 production vehicles was bulged outward from the turret.

An ammunition resupply hatch and a pistol port is provided on this side of the Panther Ausf. D. turret. Sheet metal Panzerschürzen would be suspended from the brackets attached to the upper hull sides. All hull plates were of one piece with all joints stepped, mortised and welded.

119

Vehicle "232" carried an unusual brace for the cupola hatch, allowing it to be used as a table, or as a platform for an observer. Note the shell ejection hatch in the turret side. Openings like these tended to weaken the armor, and this hatch and the side pistol ports were eliminated on the Ausführung A.

Boxes mounted on the engine compartment are raised on platforms to keep the cooling fans unobstructed. The crew's helmets are stored outside. They often had to fight their way out if the tank became disabled and MP 40 submachine guns were also carried inside.

Panther Ausf. A of 1. Abteilung, Pz. Rgt. "Grossdeutschland", during their conversion to Panthers in Belgium, early 1944. Personnel from 1./Pz.Rgt. Leibstandarte SS Adolf Hitler provide the training. They had recently converted to Panthers themselves. The tank has the new cleaning kit location on the engine deck and a triple exhaust. The two side pipes channeled air to the middle pipe, reducing the heat reaching the fuel pump and oil filter.

Panzerkampfwagen Panther, Ausf. D (Sd.Kfz. 171)

Panzerbefehlswagen (Pz.Bef.Wg.) Panther Ausf. D with binocular Turmzielfernrohr 12 sight. Unlike the earlier Pz.Kpfw. III command vehicles with fake main weapons, the Pz.Bef.Wg. Panther had a full armament and all the capabilities of the normal combat version. Later models were pre equipped with the radio mounts to convert any Panther to a command vehicle.

Well camouflaged Panther Ausf. A in Normandy, at left with Fliegerbeschußgerät (anti-aircraft) mount.

mounted on the commander cupola were standard features on this 1943 through 1944 model run. One thousand, seven hundred sixty-eight "Panthers" were produced during 1943.

The final version of the "Panther", the Ausführung G, appeared in 1944. The hull sides were considerably modified to provide improved protection for the fuel tanks. The driver vision slot in the glacis plate was eliminated and periscopes fitted instead. Toward the end of 1944, "Panthers" were fitted with the steel-rimmed running gear of the "Tiger B". Three thousand seven hundred and forty of these vehicles were produced during 1944. Total production amounted to approximately 6,000 units.

In February of 1943, the Ordnance Department had asked both Henschel and MAN to cooperate closely to create a new "Panther" which was to incorporate many features of the "Tiger II". This new vehicle, called "Panther II", was to receive, among others, a new turret, the Panzerturm "schmal". It was to carry either a 7.5 cm gun L/100 or the 8.8 cm gun L/71. Ausführung F, however, never proceeded beyond the prototype stage.

Another attempt was to mount an even smaller turret, designed by Daimler-Benz, and used for the eight-wheeled armored car, on a "Panther" chassis. The vehicle thus created was supposed to be used by reconnaissance units, but never materialized.

Panther Ausf. G fitted with 200mm Zielgerät 1221 Infrarot-Nachtsichtgerät (Infrared night sight) and 30cm searchlight for the commander. These devices were available in limited quantity at the end of 1944. The hull beginning with the Ausführung G was sloped toward the rear to protect the fuel tank locations. A rotating periscope replaced the driver's vision port.

Mid-production model of a new Panther Ausf. A with the jack moved to the vertical position between the exhaust pipes. Just underneath it is an engine access plate. To its right is a port for the manual crank start. The circular plates on both sides are track tension adjustment ports.

Pz.Kpfw. V Ausf. A ready for issue to SS-Pz.Div. "Das Reich", July 1944. Average cost upon delivery was about 117,000 Reichsmark.

125

The effectiveness of the 7,5cm KwK 42 L/70 could be fully employed in open range. Panzergranate 39/42 ammunition had an initial velocity of 925 meters per second, and the shell could penetrate 88mm of armor plate at 2,000 meters. Weights have been added to this training vehicle to represent a full combat load.

Panther Ausf. A at the APG. A barrel clamp supported the 1,500 kilogram main gun during extended travel.

Normandy, July 1944. Panther Ausf. A of 130.Panzer-Lehr-Division. Whenever possible, rail transportation was used even for short distances, otherwise the Panther consumed between 450 and 670 liters of fuel every 100 kilometers.

To communicate at the company and battalion level, extra radios and antennas were furnished to all Panzerbefehlswagen Panther Ausf. D command tanks. The isolator on the engine deck is protected by a Panzertopf (short armored housing).

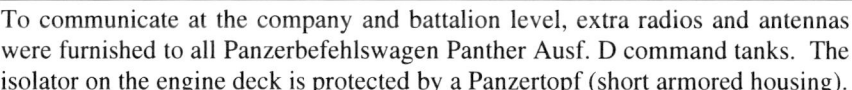

The two additional radio aerials on this Pz.Bef.Wg. Panther Ausf. D are a 'Sternantenne d' (star antenna) on the engine deck, and a 1.4m rod on the turret. The extra radio equipment reduced the number of rounds to 64.

A Panzerbefehlswagen Panther Ausf. D in the Anzio-Nettuno area, Italy. The vehicle is of 1. Abt./4. Panzer Regiment. The Elefant in the background is Oberfeldwebel Gustav Koss' vehicle of s.Pz.Jg.Abt. 653, which was disabled by a mine, late February 1944.

Befehlspanzer Panther, Ausf. D

In September 1944, Daimler-Benz introduced a steel-rimmed road wheel for 100 units of Panther Ausf. G. These reduced the problem of wheel rim bolt failures. Unfortunately, they also increased the load on the tracks, which began to break prematurely. All remaining production returned to the rubber-tired road wheels. Panther Ausf. G of Panzer Regiment 24, Aachen, November 1944.

Beginning September of 1944, later production Pz.Kpfw. V Ausf. G received a thickened turret mantlet that prevented shot from deflecting into the forward compartment.

Panther II at the Patton Museum, Fort Knox, Kentucky. Panther II carried 100mm frontal hull armor. A new turret was designed, but a standard Ausf. G turret was used to complete this captured vehicle. The turret is also retrofitted for the Infrared system.

This late Ausf. G was retrofitted for infrared installation. The anti aircraft MG ring has been deleted from the cupola and the flap trap exhaust muffler has been attached for night operations. Northern Germany, May 1945.

Panther Ausf. G of 2. Pz.Div. abandoned in Luxembourg, January 1945. The starter crank is still in place. Flammenvernichter (flame suppressing) exhausts are carried. In late 1944, a new heater for the fighting compartment was introduced, resulting in the fitting of a fan cover on the left side above the normal fan grill.

Panther Ausf. F mit "Schmalturm" (narrow turret). Two prototype models with 7,5cm KwK 44/1 L/70 were mounted on Panther Ausf. G chassis. It was designed by Rheinmetall for production by Daimler-Benz.

As the front lines neared Germany, the base mittelsand (middle sand) color was too bright for the terrain, and more olivegrün (olive drab) and rotbrun (red brown) were used.

The appreciably long 7,5cm KwK 42 L/70 had a length of 5,250 millimeters. This Panther Ausf. A of the Musée des Blindés carries the Fliegerbeschußgerät (AA mount).

Extended mud flaps are of the Ausf. D. A pair of white-tipped rods is an original feature that assisted the driver in positioning the tank. They were removed before combat.

Panzerkampfwagen V Panther Ausf. A on display at the Musée des Blindés. Power for the 8t turret was taken from the main engine shaft. When rotated manually, the hand crank only provided .36° of traverse per revolution.

Pz.Bef.Wg. Ausf. A, Panzermuseum Munster. Sweden acquired this vehicle from France in 1947, and returned it to Germany in 1961.

Panzerkampfwagen Panther, Ausf. A (Sd.Kfz. 171)

VARIATIONS

The mobility of the much-needed 8.8 cm anti-tank gun was of great concern to the German High Command. After various trials and make-shift arrangements, the "Panther" chassis was selected to serve as a basis for a completely armor-enclosed tank destroyer vehicle. The first model of this vehicle, called "Jagdpanther", was presented to Hitler on October 20, 1943. The company Mühlenbau-und lndustrie AG. (MIAG) of Braunschweig was made responsible for design and production of the vehicle. Weighing 46 metric tons, the unit mounted the long-barreled 8.8 cm Pak 43/3 L/71 in limited traverse. Mass production started at MIAG in February of 1944 and continued until the war came to an end. They were joined by Maschinenfabrik Niedersachsen-Hannover in December of 1944. Both companies completed a total of 382 "Jagdpanther" vehicles.

Krupp of Essen investigated the possibility of mounting the 12.8 cm Pak 80 L/55 in this vehicle. Only blueprints provide evidence of this undertaking.

The attempt to introduce self-propelled artillery pieces demonstrated the enormous difficulties the German armament industry was facing during the later war years. Being stretched to its very limits, it proved to be impossible to procure these important vehicles in sufficient numbers. The availability of the "Panther" chassis prompted both Krupp and Rheinmetall-Borsig to use it as a basis for self-propelled artillery vehicles. An official order by the Waffenamt in the Spring of 1942 asked both companies to create vehicles which incorporated unique features. The guns here to be made demountable from the chassis to allow their employment from the ground, while the vehicle would serve as an ammunition carrier or tank retriever. While mounted on the vehicle or on the ground, a 360° traverse was demanded. The weapons to be utilized were the 10.5 cm, leFH 43, the 12.8 cm K 43, or the 15 cm sFH 43, a heavy field artillery howitzer.

Jagdpanther (Sd.Kfz. 173) received the ZF AK 7-200 transmission. This model was more durable than that of the Panther. It had 7 forward and 1 reverse gear.

Jagdpanther of s.Pz.Jg.Abt. 560 at the APG. Late production model with two-piece barrel and bolted gun mount. This improvement allowed the barrel to be changed without removal of the entire weapon. The chassis number is 30318, produced by MNII in late 1944 and was captured in the Ardennes.

133

Though design was initiated December 1943, 'Coelian' did not enter production.

Flakpanzerwagen 341 'Coelian' prototype. Rheinmetall mounted two 3,7cm Flak 43 in a wooden mock-up turret to a Panther Ausf. D chassis.

Krupp ran all of its trials for these vehicles under the code name "Grille", while Rheinmetall-Borsig called their development "Skorpion". Daimler-Benz also got involved in this development and built, late in 1943, through the Spring of 1944, a soft-steel prototype of a weapon carrier type vehicle. Using "Panther" chassis components, it shortened each running gear by one road wheel per side. Armor was supposed to be 30 mm.

Since the limited production of the tank version of the "Panther" left no room for experimentation, these attempts soon fizzled out and were discontinued.

The same fate happened to a project started to create an AA tank based upon the "Panther". A wooden mock-up showed the installation of a 8.8 cm Flak 41 on a Panther chassis. 360° traverse and armor protection for the crew were provided. Rheinmetall worked on a similar project named "Coelian" but using the twin-mounted 3.7 cm Flak 34.

Throughout the German tank development, the trend to create armored command tanks is obvious. Vehicles used for this purpose differed only slightly from the tank version and were mainly recognizable because of their additional radio equipment indicated on the outside by additional antennas. The main armament was retained, but the ammunition stowage reduced. Two different models of the "Panther" command tank were issued to troops since 1943. The Sd. Kfz. 267 and the Sd. Kfz. 268. Both models were differentiated only by their radio equipment.

Some of the older "Panther" models were remodeled to serve as observation vehicles for staff officers and artillery observers. The main armament was removed and a dummy gun installed instead. They were called "Panzerbeobachtungswagen Panther".

Prototype of the Panzerbeobachtungswagen Panther designed for artillery observation. The turret was built of Panther Ausf. A and Ausf. D components. It was equipped with the Entfernungsmesser 1.25m rangefinder, T.B.F.2 observation periscope, T.S.R.1 spotting periscope, S.F.14Z scissors periscope, and a K.Z.F.2 telescopic gun sight. It also carried the highly effective Blockstelle 0 range plotting table, which could be used even without maps. Three radio sets were also planned, but none of the vehicles were built.

During the Allied invasion of Normandy, almost all of the Panthers in the German units that defended this sector were the older Ausführung A, and many Ausführung D models were still in service. At right, Panzerbefehlswagen Ausf. A with 2m antenna on turret roof.

Panzerbefehlswagen Ausf. A. Three elongation tubes for the Sternantenne D are below the gun cleaning kit. The unique brackets on the engine deck held spools of telephone wire.

Panzerkampfwagen Panther, Ausf. G (Sd.Kfz. 171)

Panther Ausf. A featured a cast cupola and ball-mounted MG port. The ammunition reloading hatch and pistol ports in the turret sides omitted with this version.

Example of a Panther Ausf. A. at Aberdeen Proving Ground. The number of wheel rim bolts increased over the Ausf. D from 16 to 24. These limited their failure under the weight of the vehicle.

Sheetmetal storage bins to either side of the exhausts provided a modest amount of storage for maintenance tools. Cleaning equipment for the gun is carried in the tube.

THE DEVELOPMENT OF THE PANZERKAMPFWAGEN "TIGER"

Introduction

The devastating realization of possessing inferior firepower by the German High Command shortly after the beginning of the Russian Campaign in 1941 resulted by necessity in many a make-shift solution. The only bright spot during these days of frustration was the availability of the 8.8 cm Flak antiaircraft gun. It had to be called upon to save many an impossible situation and did so sometimes under unbelievable circumstances. Used for the first time in an anti-tank role in France, this gun soon established itself in North Africa and in Russia as one of the outstanding weapons of the Second World War. Since the appearance of the Russian T-34 had made obsolete all contemporary German tank and anti-tank guns, the 8.8 cm Flak antiaircraft gun was looked upon as one of the answers to the Russian tanks. As a matter of fact, a completely new armored fighting vehicle was to evolve around this weapon, a platform adequate to provide it with a 360° traverse under strong armor protection and above average mobility. The vehicle thus created was the Tiger. Since tanks of its size, armor, and firepower had never been created before, the development of the Tiger tanks remains as one of the most fascinating accomplishments of this period.

Tiger I Ausf. E (Sd.Kfz. 181). Frontal armor thickness of 100mm compensated for the nearly vertical construction. The asymmetry of the turret is evident. This example withstood many hits.

"Tiger" Development of Dr. Ing. Porsche

Prototype VK 4501 Tiger (P) under test, April 1942. Substantial engine problems stopped production after five had been made.

A pair of Porsche Type 101/1 V-10 air-cooled engines provided power. These, in turn, drove generators, electric motors and the drive sprockets.

Professor Porsche's first attempt to create an armored fighting vehicle resulted in 1940 in a 30 ton tank which was capable of mounting either a 7.5 cm gun or a 10.5 cm main armament. Internally called type 100 or Leopard, only prototypes were actually built. They pointed in their design trends toward new avenues and brought back to reality engineering features like gasoline-electric drive components and longitudinal torsion bar suspension. Already in the spring of 1941, long before the first encounter with a new generation of Russian tanks, Porsche was asked to investigate the possibility of mounting the 8.8 cm Kwk L/56 in a tank. The turret for such a weapon was ordered by Porsche directly from Krupp of Essen, an unusual procedure, since only the Waffenamt was normally issuing production orders. As early as May 26, 1941 an official dispatch asked Porsche to accelerate this project to conform with an anticipated production start in May/June of 1942. Events in Russia lent the necessary urgency to this development.

Porsche's type 101 was ready for presentation before Hitler on April 20, 1942, but was continually plagued with mechanical problems. Especially the leak-proofing of the air-cooled main engines caused insurmountable difficulties and as a result, the entire production schedule for this vehicle was long delayed. The parallel development initiated by the Henschel Company received priority and finally the production order. In the meantime, ninety of the Porsche vehicles had been authorized for production at the Nibelungenwerke in St. Valentin, Austria. Only few were actually completed as battle tanks. They received the official name of Panzerkampfwagen VI, VK. 4501 (P), Tiger (P). Extensive research resulted in the investigation and application of advanced mechanical, electrical and hydraulic transmission components. The vehicle itself retained the gasoline-electric drive of its predecessor.

Full recognition by authorities that these vehicles could not be utilized in combat because of their mechanical unreliability, brought about a new order which transferred most of the completed chassis to the Alkett factory of Berlin-Spandau. There they were converted into heavily armored self-propelled mounts for the long barrelled 8.8 cm anti-tank gun. The original air-cooled Porsche engines were not installed and the proven water-cooled Maybach HL 120 engines substituted instead. Two engines were again necessary to propel this vehicle, which finally weighed sixty-five metric tons. The basic layout of the vehicle was modified by moving the engine compartment to the center and the main armament was mounted in limited traverse. Called Panzerjäger Tiger (P) Elefant (Sd. Kfz. 184), the completed units were issued to two battalions and saw action for the first time during the Kursk offensive in Russia in 1943. They still were hampered by mechanical difficulties and disappeared rather quickly because of battle losses and spare parts supply difficulties. Fifty of them were slightly modified by mounting commander cupolas and bow machine guns. Some of them saw further action in Italy.

Five of the chassis remaining at Nibelungenwerke were completed as tank retrievers and issued to the aforementioned tank formations. They had a closed superstructure and one ball mount machine gun for self protection. Influenced by the savage street fighting in Stalingrad, an idea was conceived, which resulted in Hitler's order to convert some of the Porsche Tiger chassis into "building demolition" vehicles. Wooden mock-up models show the vehicle with a turtle-like superstructure, mounted on a type 101 chassis, internally called the Ramm-Tiger. Equipped with a gasoline trailer to increase their radius of action, these vehicles never progressed beyond the planning stage. A similar attempt tried to mount a heavy 21 cm mortar on a Porsche Tiger chassis. This idea also soon was dropped.

Henschel VK4501(H) chassis at the proving ground with weights to represent turret load. Each hull was field tested before installing the turret. Armaments

The original production version of the Porsche Pz.Jäg. "Ferdinand," with additional bolted frontal armor. Survivors of the Kursk campaign were fitted with a hull MG 34 and modified StuG III cupola. Many later served in Italy.

Minister Albert Speer is seated center forward with Dr. Porsche at his left. The development of the turret was an independent project by Krupp.

February of 1943 saw the Waffenamt issue new orders to create a replacement vehicle for the existing Tiger vehicles. Demands to shape the hull according to the example set by the T-34 and the Panther resulted in the Porsche designs 180/181 of the VK. 4502. Running gear was similar to the Elefant, as was the power plant layout. Wegmann of Kassel had started with the construction of the new turret which was now to accommodate the 8.8 cm KwK 43 L/71. While the vehicle itself never materialized, the turret was eventually built and used for the Henschel version of the modified Tiger vehicle. Porsche's design showed various layouts, mounting the turret either in its conventional front position on the vehicle or in the rear, putting the engine compartment in between driver and fighting compartments.

Thus the entire Porsche contribution to the Tiger development consisted only of a series of prototypes never fully usable as fighting vehicles. New ideas in suspension layouts and drive-train configurations were investigated but never satisfactorily concluded.

Pz.Kpfw. VI Ausf. B Tiger II. The first production turret featured Turmzielfernrohr 9b/1 (Turret Sighting Telescope TZF9b/1) with binocular magnification 2.5 and 26° field of view.

Development of the Henschel "Tiger"

Henschel's background in tank construction dates back as far as 1933, when Henschel became involved in the production of prototypes for the Panzerkampfwagen I model run. After building various vehicles under license, this company normally known for its locomotive and truck production, started with the development of their own tank designs in 1937. Called Durchbruchwagen these prototypes utilized for the first time staggered road wheels and competed in the 30 ton weight class. During this time even a 65 ton vehicle was under consideration and actually built. Their 30 ton design, called VK. 3001 (H), was updated in 1941, to meet the new 36 to 40 ton specifications. Of the few prototypes completed, two were converted by Rheinmetall to 12.8 cm self-propelled mounts. The new vehicle, called Panzerkampfwagen IV VK. 3601, was ordered in May of 1941 and a few trial vehicles were built. They were to mount the taper-bore weapon 0725, a development ordered by Hitler as a counterpart to the Porsche vehicle. Because of the smaller turret race compared to the one used for the 8.8 cm gun, smaller vehicle dimensions and therefore reduced vehicle weights were anticipated. Since the taper-bore weapon demanded tungsten for its projectiles however, the entire project was dropped and Henschel received the order to also utilize the Krupp turret, developed for the Porsche Tiger.

Under the designation Panzerkampfwagen VI, VK. 4501 (H), Tiger (H), the VK. 3601 was redesigned to accommodate the larger turret. The superstructure was widened and the running gear improved to take care of the increased vehicle weight. The version with the Krupp turret was internally called Ausführung H 1, while a Rheinmetall design, utilizing the long 7.5 cm gun of the Panther, was called Ausführung H 2.

The prototype VK4501(H) at the Henschel Works Mittelfeld factory in Kassel, March 1942. The superstructure was welded to the hull to become one piece. The bottom plate of the hull was a single 25mm thick piece of homogenous steel, adding great rigidity to the frame. These components had been bolted together in previous designs for Panzerkampfwagen. In the background, the VK. 3001 (H) chassis.

Pz.Kpfw. VI Tiger Ausführung H (L/56). The "L/56" indicates a barrel length 56 times the diameter of its bore.

Tiger I, newly issued to Schwere Panzer Abteilung 502 (s.Pz.Abt. 502). Summer 1943.

38cm RW61 auf Sturmmörser Tiger. Only 18 were converted by Alkett from damaged Tiger I during the period August-December 1944. Two companies, Sturmmörser Kompanie 1000 and 1001 were each equipped with four vehicles in August 1944. Both units fought in the Ardennes offensive late that year.

Only wooden mock-ups of this version existed. Shown before Hitler for the first time in April of 1942, the Henschel design soon emerged as the one most suitable for mass production and without further testing production preparations commenced. In August of 1942, production started at the Mittelfeld factory of Henschel in Kassel. Originally equipped with the Maybach HL 210 twelve cylinder engine, these vehicles were first used in action near Leningrad in September, 1942. Starting with vehicle number 251, a modified version of the Maybach engine, the type HL 230, was installed, With this, the vehicles remained in production till August of 1944. A total of 1350 Panzerkampfwagen VI Tiger, Ausf. E (Sd. Kfz. 181) were built. During this production run, the original drum shaped commander cupola was replaced with a more sophisticated version. After appr. 800 of the vehicles had been completed with the original rubber tired roadwheels, a new suspension was put in production. It was based on an original Russian design used for the first time on the KV-I. Steel rimmed roadwheels with rubber inserts helped to ease somewhat the pressing raw material situation of wartime Germany.

Command tanks were always part of the German armored force. The Tiger I with additional radio equipment served this purpose. Outside appearance remained unchanged with the exception of additional antennas. Two versions of this command tank existed, the Sd. Kfz. 267 with radio sets Fu 5 and Fu 8, while Sd. Kfz. 268 had fitted the sets Fu 5 and Fu 7. Both vehicles were called Panzerbefehlswagen Tiger.

Photographic evidence shows attempts to create tank retrievers on this chassis. The vehicle, retaining its turret, had the main armament removed and carried instead a boom mounted on the top of the turret roof. This obvious make-shift arrangement existed only in a few samples. October of 1943 saw the first demonstration of the so-called Panzermörser 38 cm before Hitler. Only ten vehicles were converted from regular Tiger chassis, after having received the steel-rimmed running

Sturmpanzer VI Sturmtiger

Weighing eight more tons than Tiger I upon whose chassis it was based, Sturmpanzer VI carried a 38cm Mörser RW. 61 and dubbed "Sturmtiger". The weapon fired a variety of high explosive rocket assisted projectiles weighing several hundred kilograms. Thirteen rounds were carried, one preloaded in the tube and the remainder on racks inside.

145

gear of the late production models. A heavily armored super-structure housed a rocket launcher which was originally developed for the Navy. Interesting is the fact that while the projectiles were loaded from the inside, the recoil blast was reversed and directed through openings around the barrel toward the front of the vehicle. Alkett was responsible for the assembly of these vehicles.

The Panzerkampfwagen Tiger Ausf. E, also known as Tiger I, wrote a new chapter in armored warfare and has to be considered as quite successful considering its enormous weight and size. Despite this, Waffenamt ordered a completely new design in the fall of 1942. Henschel tried to bypass this directive in offering a Tiger I with a curved hull design, but to no avail. The new specifications for the VK. 4503 (H) asked for inclined hull plates along the lines of the Panther. The increased overall weight necessitated new major components such as steering, final drives, and running gear. Panther and Tiger main components were redesigned to be interchangeable. Main armament was originally supposed to be the 8.8 cm Flak 41, but the weapon actually developed for installation was the 8.8 cm KwK 43 which had similar ballistic performance. It was mounted in a turret originally designed for the Porsche type 180. These turrets went into production at Wegmann and were used for the first fifty production vehicles of the new Panzerkampfwagen Tiger Ausführung B (Sd. Kfz. 182). The start of production was in January of 1944 with some pre-production vehicles being built in October and December of the previous year. The Krupp production turret, affording increased armor protection and a marked decrease in production time, equipped the rest of the model run. It also allowed for the storage of additional radio sets to again create a Befehlspanzer Tiger B. War conditions allowed for only 484 Tiger B's to be completed. Seen in action for the first time in August of 1944, these vehicles never played an important part in the history of German armor.

Tiger I of s.SS-Pz.Abt. 101, 3. Kompanie. Cast cupola with seven periscopes and binocular gunsight TFZ9b classify this mid-production vehicle, carrying early pattern wheels.

Pz.Kpfw.VI Ausf. B "332" with s.Pz.Abt. 503. The first Tiger II featured 10cm of armor at the curved gun mantlet, and the turret was elevated from the deck. A Sd.Kfz. 9 FAMO 18t halftrack with crane services a vehicle in the background.

Tiger II Ausf. B (Sd.Kfz. 182) with series production turret, introduced June 1944. The turrets carried 22 rounds until a Russian ambush on 12 August 1944. Three Tiger II of s.Pz.Abt. 501 were quickly destroyed by turret penetrations that detonated the rounds.

Henschel production Jagdtiger (Sd.Kfz. 186) formerly of 3. Komp., 653 Schwere Panzerjager Abteilung. The vehicle was found March 23, 1945 by American troops on Landauer Strasse in Neustadt an der Weinstrasse.

The chassis of the Tiger B served as a basis for the heaviest armored fighting vehicle in troop use during World War II. This vehicle was the Panzerjäger Tiger Ausf. B (Sd. Kfz. 186). Mounting the 12.8 cm Pak 44 in limited traverse behind 250 mm plates, its total weight finally amounted to 75.2 metric tons. Approximately seventy of these units were delivered by Nibelungenwerke. Porsche, being responsible for the tank design at Nibelungen, tried to incorporate a chassis design of their own, the type 258. The saving in man hours for this suspension claimed by Porsche was substantial, its effectiveness however, questionable. Another Jagdtiger chassis served as a testbed for the newly created 16 cylinder air-cooled tank engine, a diesel power plant, jointly developed by Porsche and Simmering-Graz-Pauker of Vienna. Even aircraft turbines were tried.

Krupp investigated the installation of a 10.5 cm gun L/68 in the Tiger B turret utilizing a stabilized mount, while another project tried to place a longer barrelled 12.8 cm gun, namely the L/66, in a Jagdtiger. Krupp also participated in an Ordnance Department competition to utilize Tiger components for self-propelled artillery pieces.

As early as spring of 1942 specifications for a 17 cm SP gun (Gerät 5-1702) and 210 mm mortar (Gerät 5-2107) were issued. Demountability of the gun was demanded in order to achieve a 360° traverse for fire in any direction. Krupp solved this problem by putting the entire vehicle on a steel turntable which could, dismantled be carried on the vehicle itself. The demand to dismount the gun was omitted from the specifications 1944 and Krupp embarked upon the production of a prototype. This vehicle was under construction in Sennelager and was captured half finished by the British in 1945.

In regard to component design, the Tiger series was subject to many interesting developments. Torque converters, hydrostatic steering, electrical transmissions and a whole series of new power plants were envisioned, but all projects had to be cancelled because of the economic situation of the Reich.

Conclusion

It is obvious, that all efforts were being made during this time to simplify and standardize the only two remaining battle tanks, namely the Panther and the Tiger B. With all the anticipated modifications they would have been, undoubtedly, the two most advanced armored fighting vehicles of the Second World War. However, grave doubts had developed toward the end of 1944 whether or not the vehicles of the Tiger class were not already too heavy and unwieldy for logical tactical application. Even Henschel engineers admitted that the Panther was more suitable for mass production. Considering the number of man-hours per Panzer produced, the raw material shortage and the ever increasing air raids, a smaller, easier produced vehicle was most desirable.

As late as February 1945, front line officers demanded from the design department at Henschel a 35 ton battle tank, composed of already proven components. The industry, however, especially after the Allied landings in France in 1944, did not share in the hope for a successful conclusion of the war and was most reluctant to pursue any new design.

There is no doubt however, that the vehicles of the Tiger series had clearly reached the limits of what could be considered a useful fighting vehicle. Their weight and size were always a liability rather than an asset.

The 3. Kompanie of s.Pz.Abt. 503 practice with new Tiger II Ausf. B at Mailly-le-Camp, eastern France. The curved mantlet was a shot trap, but the most harm came to 3. Kompanie on August 12, 1944 when an air raid destroyed most of the tanks.

Tiger II proved themselves in open plains where the 8,8cm KwK 43 L/71 main gun could work at their maximum range of 2,000m. At that distance, and using Panzergranate 40/43 ammunition, 153mm of armor plate could be penetrated.

Early production models of Tiger I carried pistol ports each side of the turret rear. Beginning December of 1942, an escape/reloading hatch replaced the pistol port on the right side. Feifel air filters on each side of the hull were combined in a center location starting March 1943, but by December of the same year none were included. The exhaust stack shrouds were later revised to a rounded pattern. This vehicle is of s.Pz.Abt. 501 in Manuba, Tunis.

Tiger "112" was later designated "812", then "712" with 10. Pz.Div. and served last with s.Pz.Abt. 504. It was captured by American troops and is currently with the Wheatcroft collection in England.

The maintenance personnel of s.Pz.Abt. 501 moved the two headlights to these positions. Additionally, the foremost dust guards were customized. In later production Tiger I, the right headlight was omitted, and a later change moved the remaining light to the center. Tunisia, January 1943.

The angle of the hull mudguards changes direction after the first two panels to follow the true profile of the sponson. Beginning November 1942, they would be attached in one straight line. Tiger I of s.Pz.Abt. 501

Panzerkampfwagen Tiger I, Ausf. H (Sd.Kfz. 181)

©1994 UWE FEIST

Firing training of 2. Kompanie, s. Pz.Abt. 502 at Fallingbostel, spring 1943.
The 2. and 3. Kompanie had been formed in April 1943 and received new Tiger
I. By early July they would be deployed at the front.

Linking pins protrude from the spare track affixed to the turret. The track has dual center guides, each steel link connected by one pin. Ground pressure was 1.05kg/sq.cm. Grenade launchers along the perimeter of the hull were added beginning January 1943 and omitted from production in October the same year. When fired, these would explode 1-2 meters out and release 360 steel balls.

The bocage of Normandy reduced the opportunity to fire at long-range, and losses were heavy. This Tiger I Ausf. E is a replacement vehicle with 9. s.Komp./SS-Pz.Rgt. 3, which was furnished in the summer of 1944.

Tiger I Ausf. E "A 12" of 3. Panzer Regiment Grossdeutschland has just received transportation track in preparation for rail transit, leaving behind the wider combat track. The late production steel-rimmed wheels did not have to be removed for the change. Gumbinnen, East Prussia, late July 1944.

Normandy, 1944. Tiger "232" commanded by SS-Unterscharführer Kurt Kleber, s.SS-Pz.Abt. 101.

A captured British Daimler scout car leads Tiger I "211". A 200-liter drum of fuel is carried to extend range.

Tiger I of s.Pz.Abt. 503 in Bourgtheroulde during the retreat toward the Seine River. This is a late production version with cast cupola, small muzzlebrake and single aperture in the mantlet for the TZF9c monocular gunsight.

Late-production Tiger I Ausf. E "211" of 2. Kompanie, s.SS-Pz.Abt. 102. From February 1944, the road wheels were a pressed steel type, mounted two per swing arm, instead of three as before. In addition, the idler wheel was changed to a smaller diameter, and the twice the number of bolts attached the new wheels to the hubs.

A heavy tank battalion of three companies was created for Panzer Grenadier Division Grossdeutschland as the III.Abteilung, Panzer Regiment Grossdeutschland. This Tiger I is the company commander's vehicle of 10. Kompanie. The first company (9. Kompanie) was created from the original 13.Kompanie. The second and third companies (10 and 11 Kompanien) were the former 3.Kompanie of s.Pz.Abt. 501 and 3.Kompanie of s.Pz.Abt. 504, respectively. The headquarters (Stab), 10 and 11 Kompanien joined 9.Kompanie at the front on 14 August 1943.

Panzerkampfwagen Tiger I, Ausf. H (Sd.Kfz. 181)

Panzerkampfwagen VK 4501 (P) (Porsche Prototype)

Panzerkampfwagen Tiger I (Sd.Kfz. 181)

Prototype Tiger II. The cupola has a pistol port, with conical plug. A reloading hatch just below was installed in the first vehicles. This unit also has narrow transportation tracks. The leading segment of the track apron can be folded inwards for rail transit, but this design was not adopted for production.

Apart from five issued to the "Feldherrnhalle"' Division in March 1945, the balance of Tiger II went to independent schwere Panzer detachments of the Wehrmacht and the Waffen SS.

This particular vehicle was issued to the Panzerversuchsstelle (tank testing facility) at Kummersdorf in the spring of 1944. Recovering the 68-ton Tiger II from this training position is a difficult prospect.

Panzerkampfwagen Tiger II, Ausf. B (Porsche Turm)

Tiger II (Fahrgestell Nr. 280243) produced September 1944. It was assigned to s.SS-Pz.Abt. 501 and part of Kampfgruppe Peiper in the Ardennes battles. It was abandoned near Trois-Pont, Belgium and captured by American troops 24 December 1944. These are the original wartime colors.

162

This vehicle is prepared for travel with removal of the Panzerschürzen and fitting of transportation tracks for rail transport. The massive combat tracks weighed 3t each, and their design evolved in at least four iterations through the course of production.

A coaxial MG 34 supplements the 8,8cm KwK 43 L/71. After April of 1944, a portion of the upper front glacis plate was removed in front of the radio operator, as on the driver's side, for better visibility.

Henschel Tiger II of the commander of 3. Kompanie, s.Pz.Abt. 503. The crew is reattaching the Panzerschürzen after painting the vehicle. The loader's hatch was augmented in thickness from 1,5cm to 4cm with the production turret.

Tiger "112" formerly of the collection at Aberdeen Proving Grounds. It [ ] been on display at the Sinsheim Technical Museum, Deutsches Panzer Muse[ ] Munster, and is now at the Wheatcroft collection.

The only running example of the Tiger II is at the Musée des Blindés. It is m[ ] up of the components of no less than five other scavenged vehicles. The Mayb[ ] HL230P30 engine was governed to 2500rpm, and at 2000rpm, the turret co[ ] rotate at 19° per second.

This Tiger II served in France with s.SS-Pz.Abt. 501. It was made by Hensche[ ] July 1944 and was one of three knocked out near Beauvais and taken Septem[ ] 1944 by the US Army. It was returned to Germany as a gift in December of 19[ ] It is shown here at Panzermuseum Munster about the same time.

Panzerkampfwagen Tiger II, Ausf. B "Königstiger" (Sd.Kfz. 182)

Jagdtiger

Armed with the 12,8cm Panzerjägerkanone 44 L/55, the Jagdtiger was able to destroy any allied armor in the field even at ranges beyond 2000 meters. Two suspension arrangements were produced, and this example is of the Henschel type with larger road wheels. The vehicle weighed 70.6-tons and consumed up to 12 liters of fuel per kilometer traveled. The example is seen here at Aberdeen Proving Ground and is Fahrgestell #305020, produced in October of 1944.

Panzerlehrgang Mielau, 1944. Due to their weaker Type 258 suspensions, Porsche Jagdtiger were initially used for training, but as the need arose they were assigned to combat operations. The paired road wheel assemblies were welded to the hull and prone to breaking off, unlike the Henschel version with penetrating torsion bars. This vehicle is Fahrgestell Nr. 305003.

Jagdtiger enroute for assignment to s.Pz.Jg.Abt. 653, Fahrgestell Nr. 305009. Narrow tracks are fitted and the side skirts and tow ropes have been removed for rail transport.

A thin skirt protected each exhaust, preventing contact with the hot pipe and reducing visible glow at night. Armor thickness at hull and superstructure rear was 80mm. Fahrgestell Nr. 305003, with track of the Elephant type.

Jagdpanzer VI "Jagdtiger" (12,8 cm Pak) (Sd.Kfz. 186)

Sturmpanzer VI "Sturmtiger" (38 cm Mörser)

STURMARTILLERIE

In 1934, the basic concept of the newly developed "Panzerka-mpfwagen" provided a clear indication of their main purpose: namely, to be used within Armored Divisions for operational warfare. The infantry, which was left without armored support, demanded a vehicle of their own. Agreeing with their demand, the German High Command placed an order on June 15, 1936 to create an armored vehicle to be used as support artillery for assault and anti-tank purposes.

Charged with the responsibility for design and development were the companies of Daimler-Benz AG. of Berlin-Marienfelde for chassis and superstructure and Friedrich Krupp AG. of Essen for the armament. In its final design, the vehicle appeared as a full-tracked, turretless, fully enclosed armored vehicle, mounting a short barreled 7.5 cm Kwk L/24 (the main armament of the Panzer IV) in limited traverse. To accommodate these features, including a four man crew and armor protection of 10 to 50 mm, a Panzer III chassis was used.

After exhaustive research, between 1937 and 1939 an 0-series of 30 vehicles was authorized with production starting in February of 1940. Six of these vehicles were field tested during the campaign in France in 1940.

The first production model, called "Ausführung A" carried the official designation: Gepanzerte Selbstfahrlafette für Sturmgeschütz 7.5 cm (Sd. Kfz. 142). Based upon the chassis of the Panzer III Ausf. F (5/ZW), the vehicle had a total weight of 19.6 metric tons. Delivery started on August 2, 1940. Responsible for assembly at that time was the Altmärkische Kettenfabrik GmbH. (Alkett) of Berlin-Spandau. The

Sturmgeschütz III Ausf. A. The 7,5cm StuK37 L/24 was offset right to provide space for the driver. The armor of the gunsight trough was stepped to deflect incoming fire.

Sturmgeschütz Ausf. B of the Artillerie-Lehrregiment (ALR) at Truppenübungsplatz Jüterbog (training camp), 1940.

170

Sturmgeschütz were a welcome sight for infantry, and their tactical supporting role was continually refined. The roof of the Ausführung B (Sd.Kfz. 142) was modified to allow the gunner's periscope to emerge.

Italy, February 1944. A StuG III Ausf. F/8 of "Hermann Göring" Panzer Division. With this version the rear deck was elongated lengthwise. The engine air intake design was improved with raised armored housings like those introduced with the Pz.Kpfw. III Ausf. L. In addition, rear hull armor thickness was increased from 30mm to 50mm.

models B, C, D and E followed during 1941 and 1942 based upon the Panzer III Ausf. H (7/ZW). There were only insignificant differences between these models. The production start of Ausf. C was in June, 1941.

After the appearance of the Russian T-34 in 1941, Hitler demanded on September 28th an increase in armor protection and a high velocity gun for the Sturmgeschütz. Daimler-Benz was again contracted to improve the chassis, while Rheinmetall-Borsig AG. of Düsseldorf developed a modified superstructure and provided a long barreled gun. Official presentation of this model to Hitler took place on March 31, 1942.

Production commenced for these most needed vehicles in spring of 1942. The new assault gun, named now the "Sturmgeschütz 40" (Ausf. F) (Sd. Kfz. 142/1) mounted the 7.5 cm Sturmkanone 40 L/43. Armor was still 50 mm, the total weight now 21.6 metric tons.

One hundred nineteen of these vehicles were built. Starting with unit 120, the 7.5 cm Sturmkanone 40 in its final length of L/48 was installed. The official designation was now "Sturmgeschütz 40" (Ausf. F/8).

The final version of the Sturmgeschütz appeared by the end of 1942. Frontal armor was now increased to 80 mm. An improved superstructure was fitted with a commander's cupola and a MG 34 or 42 for close-battle protection. Equipped in production with the standard armor skirts, these vehicles were now also built by Daimler-Benz and Miag of Braunschweig, proved to be most efficient in protecting infantry against enemy armor. Official documents credit Sturmgeschütz units for the destruction of 20,000 enemy tanks by spring of 1944. Production figures for 1943, 1944 and 1945 indicate 3041, 4850 and 145 Sturmgeschütz as having been built during this time.

Beginning with StuG III Ausf. E, a pannier was fitted to both sides of the superstructure. This long armored box on the left side fit both the radio (FuG15 and additional six rounds for the main gun. With the extra radio equipment, the StuG III Ausf. E could replace the Sd.Kfz. 253 half-track in the command role.

StuG III Ausf. B being resupplied by a Sd.Kfz. 252 Munitionsträger. A combination of 44 rounds of armor piercing and high explosive ammunitio rounds were carried for the 7,5cm StuK37 L/24 main gun.

A crew intercommunication system was introduced with the StuG III Ausf. D These vehicles are of 5. Geschütz, 2./ Sturmartillerie Abteilung 190. Greece April 1941.

Sturmgeschütz III (7,5 cm) Ausf. C and D (Sd.Kfz. 142)

Sturmgeschütz 40 Ausf. G with late production features: "Saukopfblende" cast mantle with coaxial MG 34, barrel clamp, Rundumfeuer (remote control) machine gun and shot deflector in front of the commander's cupola. Fahrgestell Nr. 107546 manufactured by Alkett late 1944.

Beginning with the Sturmgeschütz III Ausf. F, the upper superstructure was angled more steeply to meet the edge of the roof. Vehicle of the 3.Batterie StuG Abteilung "Grossdeutschland", Russia, April 1943.

Sturmgeschütz III Ausf. G of 2. Batterie, Sturmgeschütz Brigade 243 on the Eastern Front, 1943. The superstructure of the StuG III Ausf. G was widened and the cupola added for the commander. Beginning December 1942, a shield was provided for the loader's machine gun station.

7,5 cm Sturmgeschütz 40 (Sd.Kfz. 142/1) Ausf. G

The installation of the long barreled gun indicated a basic change in the role of these support vehicles. To assure infantry units support against other than enemy armor, the 10.5 cm Sturmhaubitze 42 (Sd. Kfz. 142/2) was issued to Sturmgeschütz formations. Basically unchanged, these vehicles mounted a 10.5 cm howitzer instead of the 7.5 cm gun. The production target asked for 24 of these units per month. Originally the gun was equipped with a muzzle brake, which was later omitted due to supply difficulties. The initial model was based upon the Sturmgeschütz Ausf. F, while the final version was called Ausführung G.

Vehicles of this type, but without gun, were used in small numbers as ammunition carriers or "Munitionspanzer III".

To mount the sIG 33, a heavy infantry howitzer, twelve Panzer III chassis were utilized in 1941. Weighing 21 tons, these vehicles with a crew of five and mounting the 15 cm Howitzer L/11 carried the designation: Sturm-infanterie-Geschütz 33. Owing to the limited payload capacity of the Panzer III chassis, adequate armor protection could not be provided and the task of this vehicle was taken over by the Panzer IV mounted Sd. Kfz. 166 "Brummbär".

After the Panzer IV production at Krupp-Gruson in Magdeburg was relocated to the Nibelungenwerke in St. Valentin, Austria, the available production capacity was converted toward the production of the Sturmgeschütz IV. The superstructure of this assault gun was almost identical to the one of the Sturmgeschütz III. Only the driver front was altered to accommodate the Panzer IV chassis. With a four man crew and frontal armor of 80 mm, the fighting weight was 23,000 kp (23 ton).

Since fall of 1943 these vehicles, together with the Sturmgeschütz III, comprised the main equipment of Sturmgeschütz outfits and partially also of tank units.

Over 1,200 of the 10,5cm Sturmhaubitze 42 were issued to Panzerjäger units. They were employed against hardened targets. This vehicle, of Sturmgeschütz Brigade 322, is seen in October 1944 carrying Russian prisoners of war.

Generalfeldmarschall Albert Kesselring is given a firing demonstration atop this Sturmgeschütz IV. Italy, 1944.

176

13269
9.3.42.

Sturmgeschütz III Ausf. F (Sd.Kfz. 142/1) with 7,5cm StuK40 L/43. The work was completed at the Altmärkische Kettenwerk Gmbh (Alkett) Werke, Berlin Falkensee from Fahrgestell Nr. 91401 to 93850. The 7,5cm StuK40 L/43 was mounted in the first 120 Ausf. F, after which an L/48 was installed. A fume extracting ventilation fan was added on the roof.

This prototype of the 10,5cm Sturmhaubitze 42 (Sd.Kfz. 142/2) used the Ausf. F chassis and modified Ausf. E superstructure. The powerful leichte Feldhaubitze 18 was aimed by the Sfl.Z.F.1a gunsight with 5x magnification and an 8° field of view. Maximum sight range was 2,000 meters. A total of 36 rounds were carried.

178

10,5 cm Sturmhaubitze 42, Ausf. F (Sd.Kfz. 142/2)

The first nine 10,5cm Sturmhaubitze were completed by October 1942. In November, they were sent to Leningrad to 3.Batterie/ Sturmgeschütz-Abteilung 185.

179

13276
9.3.42

Series production of the Sturmhaubitze began in October 1942 using StuG III Ausführung F, Ausf. F/8 and Ausf. G chassis. By February of 1945, 1,211 units had been completed. For the Kursk campaign, 68 were assigned to Army Groups Center and South. After September 1944 the muzzle brake was omitted. Armor thickness was 30mm at hull sides.

Captured in Italy. 10,5cm Sturmhaubitze 42 at Aberdeen Proving Ground. The bracket on the hull front held the missing NOTEK light.

A 7,5cm StuG 40 Ausf. G at APG features 30mm of bolted armor plate to augment the basic 50mm thickness. The hull sides extend to create towing locations at the front, and the fenders are shorter and not hinged as before.

Krupp-Grusonwerk factory in Magdeburg. Thirty Sturmgeschütz IV were completed in December of 1943. These helped fill a shortfall that had been incurred by the bombing of the Alkett factory and production of the StuG III.

Evidence of the original StuG III superstructure: bolted armor to the right of the gun (50mm+30mm). This was superceded in later production by a single plate 80mm thick.

Serrated frames were designed to hold late-pattern Panzerschürzen. These allowed any caught panels to lift and release in either direction.

Sturmgeschütz IV weighed 1 ton less than StuG III and had a greater fuel range (156 vs. 210 km). The single plate frontal armor was also more effective than the original bolted combination.

Italy, 1943. A familiarization course for Commonwealth troops on German and Italian self-propelled Panzerjäger. Note the commander's cupola shot deflector on the StuG IV. Italian Semovente da 105/25 complete the collection in the background.

Sturmgeschütz IV based on Pz.Kpfw. IV Ausf. J chassis with vertical exhaust stacks.

Jagdpanzer IV, Ausf. F (Sd.Kfz. 162)

Jagdpanzer IV Ausf. F (Sd.Kfz. 162) O-Serienfahrzeug. The chassis of the Pz.Kpfw. IV Ausf. F furnished a reliable platform for Jagdpanzer development. This initial production vehicle featured 60mm of frontal armor and 30mm at the sides. This was later increased in May 1944 to 80mm at front and 40mm at the sides. Both the 7,5cm Pak39 L/43 and L/48 were used.

Sturmgeschütz IV (7,5cm StuK40 L/48) (Sd.Kfz. 167) combined a Pz.Kpfw. IV chassis with a Sturmgeschütz III Ausf. G superstructure. The driver's compartment was elongated.

Jagdpanzer IV (7,5cm StuK42 L/70) was nose heavy due to the overhang of the gun and heavy frontal armor. Steel road wheels at this end were substituted and three return rollers instead of four were installed. A barrel clamp would be introduced to steady the gun during travel.

As a replacement for the Sturmgeschütz IV, the Panzerjäger IV was created. Designed and built by Vomag AG. of Plauen/ Vogtland, these vehicles also utilized the chassis of the Panzer IV (Ausf. F). It appeared as a turretless tank destroyer with ballistically well sloped armor of 60 mm frontal strength. The total height was only 1860 mm. Normally with a four man crew, the unit weighed 24 tons. As a commander's vehicle the crew was increased to five carrying an additional radio operator and mounting a MG 34 in the sloping front plate of the hull. Main armament was still the 7.5 cm Pak 39 L/48 with or without muzzle brake. Officially named: Panzerjäger IV Ausf. F (Sd. Kfz. 162). Demonstrated for the first time on March 14, 1943 production commenced on October 20th of the same year. During the first part of 1944, Vomag investigated the installation of the 7.5 cm Panzerjägerkanone 42 L/70 (main armament of Panzerkampfwagen Panther) in the Jagdpanzer IV. After several prototypes, the final version went into production by mid-year 1944. It appeared with front units by August 1944. Officially known as "Panzer IV/70" (Sd. Kfz. 162/1), this vehicle looked almost identical to the Panzerjäger IV, Ausf. F. it mounted, however, the 7.5 cm Sturmkanone 42 L/70 and had 80 mm frontal armor. Total weight was 25.8 tons. Maneuverability was impaired since the long gun and the increase in frontal armor put too much weight to the front of the vehicle. The final series of these tank destroyer vehicles had a modified suspension system in having only three return rollers instead of the usual four. Guderian himself was not at all convinced of the necessity for such a vehicle. He considered the Panzerjäger IV with the 7.5 cm L/48 to be quite adequate. Production for both versions totalled 1530 units in 1944.

There existed a constant demand by infantry units for a high explosive-shell weapon which could be used in close support roles. Available to them for years was the so-called heavy infantry Howitzer 33 (sIG 33), which was mounted, in order to provide mobility, over the years on Panzer I, II, 38 (t) and

Jagdpanzer IV (Sd.Kfz. 162) of 116. Panzer Division, 3.Komp., 228. Pz.Jg.Abt. France, 1944.

Many Jagdpanzer IV were not furnished with the muzzle brake. The low 1.86m profile is about even with the height of the soldier.

186

Jagdpanzer IV, Ausf. F (Sd.Kfz. 162)

Marinovka, Russia, 1943. The Sturminfanteriegeschütz 33B was based on a Pz.Kpfw.III chassis and mounted a 15cm StuIG L/11.

Only 24 StuIG33B were produced. One company fought in Stalingrad while another company of StuIG with 23. Pz.Div. participated in the relief attempt of 6. Armee.

The robust SturmInfanteriegeschütz 33 carried 80mm of frontal armor in a superstructure designed to contain the 15cm sIG 33 and protect the crew from the perils of street fighting.

The 21-ton vehicle carried a crew of five, 30 rounds of howitzer ammunition, and 600 rounds of ammunition for the MG 34 machine gun.

SIG 33 assigned to Panzer Regiment 201, 23. Panzer Division. The development period for the vehicle was a scant 14 days, and refinements such as a proper cupola were left out.

These Sturmpanzer Pz.Kpfw. III Ausf. N are of s.Pz.Abt. 501, Tunisia 1943,
where they supported the Tiger I in the battalion. Later models replaced the
split hatch cupola and paired turret doors with single pieces.

Pz.Kpfw.III Ausf. N (7,5 cm Stuk)

Sturmpanzer Pz.Kpfw. III, Ausf. N mit 7,5cm StuK. L/24 (Sd.Kfz. 141/2). Spaced armor was introduced in March 1943 for the turret and hull sides. It was not used on the mantlet as with earlier models due to the weight of the main weapon.

Jagdpanzer IV Ausf. F (Sd.Kfz. 162). Conical plugs cover the two MG ports. After March 1944, only the port left of the main gun was retained. The hull front consists of interlocking welded plate. The 7,5cm Pak39 L/48 was hand traversed and could move 12° either side with elevation range +15° and –8°. It is offset right by 20cm to create room for the driver and gunner.

The simplified idler wheels are of tube steel with welded support flanges in between. The idlers were also adjustable and the Kgs. 61/400/120 track was tensioned at these points. A round door above the muffler allowed the pulley driving the water pump, oil cooler, generator, and fan drive to be disengaged.

193

Panzerkampfwagen III (7,5 cm) Ausf.N (Sd.Kfz. 141/2)

Alkett in Berlin Spandau built a prototype vehicle of a Panzerjäger with 7,5cm Pak 42 L/70. It was designated Panzer IV/70(A) Übergangslösung and based on the Pz.Kpfw. IV Ausf. J chassis. It was not adopted for production.

Assembled by VOMAG, the Panzer IV/70(V) debuted with Wehrmacht Independent Panzer Brigades 105 and 106 in the Ardennes region of Belgium, December 1944. The 7,5cm Pak 42 L/70 was built by the two firms of Gustloff-Werke in Weimar, and Skoda in Pilsen. This weapon replaced the shorter Pak 39 L/48 of the early Pz.Jäg. IV. A barrel clamp on the hull front was required to secure the weapon during travel.

Panzer IV/70(V) (Sd.Kfz. 162/1) were based on a simplified Pz.Kpfw. IV Ausf. F chassis. The face-hardened armor plate was produced by Witkowitzer Bergbau und Eisenhütten AG.

III chassis. In all cases the armor protection proved to be inadequate. In its final form, based upon the Panzer IV chassis, the vehicle was sufficiently armored (up to 100 mm) and carried with a crew of five, the 15 cm Sturmhaubitze 43 L/12. Total weight was 28.2 metric tons. Designated as "Sturmpanzer 43 Brummbär", it carried the Sd. Kfz. 166. Developed by Alkett of Berlin, the assembly line was at the Deutsche Eisen Werke in Duisburg. Approximately 60 of these vehicles were issued to fighting units starting in April of 1943.

One of the most reliable tank chassis, used by the German army during World War II, was the one of the Czech Panzer 38 (t) built by Praga. It was only natural to utilize these chassis components for a "Sturmgeschütz" type vehicle. As a result, the Jagdpanzer 38 "Hetzer" was created. Small in its outside dimensions, mounting a 7.5 cm Pak 39 L/48 and weighing only 16 tons, this vehicle was one of the most versatile and advanced tank destroyer designs of World War II. It had a frontal armor, 60 mm thick, well sloped, and a crew of four.

Built by Praga of Prague and later on also by Skoda, Werk Königsgrätz. The Swiss army purchased 158 units during 1946 and 1947. Total production was approximately 3000. The same vehicle, equipped with a flame-thrower instead of the gun, was issued to special units as "Flammwerferpanzer 38". Only few of these units were produced as was a very similar tank retriever called "Bergepanzer 38".

Intended for its replacement in 1945 was the "Panzerjäger 38 (d)", which was supposed to enter troop service as the light standard armored vehicle of the Wehrmacht. Almost identical in its appearance to the "Jagdpanzer 38", this new tank destroyer vehicle was equipped with an air-cooled 210 HP Tatra diesel engine. Original drawings dated February, 1945 indicated two versions to be produced:

This Sturmpanzer IV is the first version with a Fahrersehklappe 80 visor for the driver, similar to the Tiger I. There is no secondary armament, only pistol ports in the hull sides.

Jagdpanzer 38(t) für 7,5cm Pak 39. This is the late model with the front corners of the side skirts angled inward to avoid snagging vegetation. The mantlet was also widened over the first version. This vehicle is currently at The Tank Museum, Bovington, UK.

The first production Jagdpanzer 38 in front of the factory of the Böhmisch-Mährischen-Maschinenfabrik, Prague, March 1944. Though it was based on a widened Czech 38(t) chassis, the suspension was strengthened to handle the heavy nose armor and weapon. The first three prototypes were tested extensively for a month, and the type was accepted for production as replacement for all existing interim solutions.

197

Sturmpanzer IV Brummbär

The Sturmpanzer IV "Brummbär" mit 15cm Sturmhaubitze 43 L/12 underwent several refinements during its production run. This example succeeded the initial version with a modified driver compartment; in place of a forward looking visor, a rotating periscope was provided. This strengthened the armor plate.

The HL 120 TRM engine handled the 3 tons of additional weight over the Pz.Kpfw. IV for which it was designed. The widened superstructure displaced the former storage space above the fenders. This was remedied with racks of spare wheels and the large box of track adjustment tools.

Jagdpanzer V "Jagdpanther" (8,8 cm Pak) (Sd.Kfz. 173)

Sturmpanzer IV "Brummbär" (15 cm StuH) (Sd.Kfz. 166)

An early Jagdpanther (Sd.Kfz. 173) seen during training at Mailly-le-Camp. The type is characterized by single-piece barrel and recessed mantlet. It is with schwere Panzerjäger Abteilung 654.

Panzerjäger 38 (d) (W 1807) - Engine in rear of vehicle

Panzerjäger 38 (d) (W 1806) - Engine in center of vehicle

Suggested main armament was the 7.5 cm Panzerjägerkanone 42 L/70. The development of this vehicle received top priority during 1944/45. Production capacities were made available from former Panzer IV facilities. The monthly production schedule asked for 2000 of these units. Included in this figure were between 300 to 350 armored weapons carrier vehicles and some reconnaissance units. Production, however, was never started since the war was at that time in its closing stages.

Climaxing the development of German tank destroyer vehicles during World War II, not so much in dimensions but in effectiveness, was the "Jagdpanther". The mobility of the much used and most effective long barreled 8.8 cm anti-tank gun left in its previous solutions as a self-propelled mount much to be desired. Neither the "Nashorn", based upon the Panzer III/IV chassis with its inadequate armor protection, nor the "Elefant", based upon the Porsche Tiger chassis with its very elaborate chassis design, provided a satisfactory solution.

In merging the very modern chassis design of the "Panther" tank with the outstanding ballistic performance of the 8.8 cm Pak 43 L/71 and surrounding it with well sloped armor of 80 mm frontal strength, a vehicle was conceived which ranked among the best anti-tank weapons of its time. One of its few drawbacks was its excessive weight of 46 metric tons.

Shown as a model for the first time on October 20, 1943 and developed by the company Mühlenbau und Industrie AG. (Miag) of Braunschweig, the vehicle entered troop service in March of 1944. Officially known as "8.8 cm Pak 43/3 auf Panzerjäger Panther" (Sd. Kfz. 173) or "Jagdpanther", the vehicle was also assembled by Maschinenfabrik Niedersachsen-Hannover of Hannover. Production at MNH started in December 1944. Both companies produced a total of 384 units. Panzerjäger vehicles, using both the Tiger B (Jagdtiger), Tiger (P) chassis (Porschetiger)

They closed the gap, however, and provided hard-pressed infantry units with much-needed protection. This was especially true during the initial phase of the Russian Campaign in 1941, when Russian tanks, and specifically their "T-34", rendered the entire German tank and anti-tank weaponry useless. During this period, only the 8.8 cm Flak antiaircraft gun, never intended to be used at that scale for ground support, proved to be effective. To equalize the balance of fire power, every conceivable weapon was utilized, and it will be most difficult to mention all of the conversions within the framework of this book.

8,8cm Pak 43/3 auf Pz.Jäg. Panther. These Jagdpanther of s.Pz.Jg.Abt. 654 make way out of Normandy near Bourgtheroulde toward the Seine River. Top speed was 46 km/h on good roads, but the second vehicle is being towed.

In order to make it easier for the reader to comprehend the material offered, we shall use the vehicle chassis as a basis and list the armament for better identification in the following sequence:

Self-propelled anti-tank guns
Self-propelled artillery pieces
Self-propelled antiaircraft guns

Self-propelled guns in support of armored formations were tried without too much enthusiasm and success in many an army during the late Twenties and early Thirties. None of them actually reached mass-production stage during this time. Artillery pieces were mostly truck or tractor-drawn, a solution considered quite adequate for mechanized warfare.

Jagdtiger mit 12,8cm Pak 44 L/55. From the total of 77 vehicles, the few manufactured by Porsche carried this Type 258 suspension of welded bogie assemblies.

4,7cm Pak(t) (Sf) auf Pz.Kpfw. I Ausf. B. Alkett vehicle with five-sided 14,5mm shield. Others produced by Skoda had a seven-sided compartment. The concept was successful but this particular weapon was quickly outclassed because of the small caliber weapon.

15cm sIG33 L/11.4 (Sf) auf Pz.Kpfw. I Ausf. B. Known as Bison, only 38 were converted January-February 1940 by Alkett. The entire sIG 33 field carriage was mounted. The additional 2,700 kg overburdened the chassis.

The revolution of warfare demonstrated by armored divisions during the initial stage of World War II, however, changed the old views rapidly. Too often armored units found themselves left without the vital support of infantry and artillery, since the soft-skinned vehicles of these units were too vulnerable to ground and aircraft attacks.

A solution to provide armor protection for these support elements had to be found immediately and resulted quite often in makeshift arrangements, using in most cases outdated battle tank chassis no longer suited for combat.

The beginning of this most interesting development was made already in 1939 and 1940, when the first conversions of the obsolete Panzer I appeared with front units. ALKETT, Berlin converted 132 Panzer I chassis to tank destroyer vehicles. Called "4.7 cm Pak (t) auf Panzerkampfwagen I (Sd. Kfz. 101) ohne Turm", these vehicles carried the Czech 47 mm anti-tank gun behind 14.5 mm armor plate. With a three-man crew, their total weight was 6.4 metric tons. The units saw service in France, Africa, and Russia, where they rapidly disappeared because of their inadequate fire power.

Also converted by Alkett were 38 "15 cm sIG 33 auf Panzerkampfwagen I (Gw I)", a clumsy-looking vehicle which was meant to support Infantry units. They were also used up rather quickly during the first month of the Russian Campaign. In France, however, they proved the soundness of this new concept and opened the door to a vast conglomeration of self-propelled support vehicles.

Quite identical in weight was a little-known conversion based upon the Borgward-built ammunition carrier VK 301. The official order for this vehicle was issued in July, 1940. Two prototypes were built by Rheinmetall of Düsseldorf and equipped with the 5 cm Pak 38 (Main armament of the late model Panzer III). These units were field-tested and soon abandoned because even the 5 cm weapon was inadequate

The Panzerjäger I was armed with a 4,7cm Pak(t) and could carry 86 rounds of ammunition for the anti tank gun. An MP 40 was available (1,920 rounds) for the 3 man crew.

Powered by a 100 horsepower Maybach 6-cylinder engine, the 6,4t vehicle consumed 125 liters of gasoline per 100 km road travel.

Alkett utilized the obsolete chassis of the Pz.Kpfw. I Ausführung B to create the 4,7cm Pak(t) auf Panzerkampfwagen I (Sd.Kfz. 101). Skoda furnished the superstructure shields of seven sides. A total of 132 units were built from 1939 until late 1940.

Rearview of the Panzerjäger I. A total of 132 units were built from 1939 until late 1940.

Bison of 704 schwere Infanteriegeschütz Abteilung, with 10 Pz. Div, France, May 1940. Vehicles of this unit where later attached to 5. Pz. Div. and ended their service in Russia, mid-1943.

15 cm sIG33 auf Pz.Kpfw. I Ausf. B "Bison" with 1. Panzer Division in France. A shield of a modest 10mm thickness was attached to form the fighting compartment.

Weapon elevation of -4° to +75° was possible, with traverse of 12.5° in each direction. Note the Rblf36 gun sight and protective wicker cocoons for the 15 cm rounds. One shell was carried on the right fender and two on the left.

against the Russian T-34. Very interesting is the fact that Rheinmetall received a follow-up order by the Ordnance Department in September, 1941, to replace the 5 cm Pak with a 10.5 cm recoilless rifle. Only one wooden mock-up was completed.

The initial Panzer II conversion also carried the 5 cm Pak. Using the F version of the regular light tank, 44 units were converted but soon re-equipped with the 75 mm AT gun. Parallel to the above-mentioned VK. 301, a similar conversion was made with the VK. 901, a prototype of the Panzer II development. Called the "Panzer Selbstfahrlafette lc", only two vehicles mounting the 5 cm Pak were field-tested and suffered the same fate as the VK. 301.

On December 20, 1941, an emergency order was issued to create, under a crash program, a tank destroyer vehicle using captured Russian 7.62 cm AT and field guns and the chassis of the Panzer II D and E. This version of the Panzer II was originally supposed to be the main equipment of the "Light Divisions" and was later converted into flame-thrower tanks. They had, unlike the normal Panzer II, four large road wheels on either side mounted on torsion bars. Alkett converted 150 to SP tank destroyers and called them "Panzer Selbstfahrlafette I für 7.62 cm Pak 36 (r) (Sd. Kfz. 132) Marder II". Limited availability of this chassis resulted in an order dated May, 1942, to utilize now obsolete chassis of the other Panzer II models. Alkett built a total of 1217, with production beginning in June of 1942. Officially known as "7.5 cm Pak 40/2 auf. Sfl. II (Sd. Kfz. 131) Marder II", these vehicles, despite their open superstructure, provided most effective anti-tank protection in Russia.

In their initial attempt to supply armored artillery units with SP vehicles, the German High Command had in mind to create a unique design. They specified all-round traverse and demountability of the armament. The fact remains, however, that all these well-meant intentions had to be abandoned

Pz. Selbstfahrlafette I für 7,62cm Pak36(r) auf Fahrgestell Pz.Kpfw. II Ausf. D1, D2 (Sd.Kfz 132). These vehicles were built from Pz.Kpfw. II that had been returned from combat for repair or conversion.

7,5cm Pak 40/2 auf Fahrgestell Pz.Kpfw. II (Sf) (Sd.Kfz.131). Seen in Russia, Marder II were issued to Panzerjäger units from July 1942. A total of 1,217 units were built by MAN and Alkett.

207

Using obsolete Panzer II Ausf. A/B/C and Ausf. F chassis, the Selbsfahrlafette für 7,5 cm Pak 40/2 (Sd.Kfz. 131) "Marder" was created. A crew of three manned the vehicle, which also carried 37 rounds of ammunition for the main gun. Traverse was asymmetrical at 32° left and 25° right. This example was at Aberdeen Proving Ground for many years and is currently at the Wheatcroft Collection in England.

Panzerjäger (7,5 cm Pak) auf Fgst. Pz.II "Marder II"

An Oberfeldwebel stands in the fighting compartment of his Panzerjäger. Several minor changes to the superstructure and shields were made in different production runs, and a weapon traverse of 50 degrees in either direction was achieved. The muzzle brake was added to the gun to slightly improve the accuracy.

Men of the Fallschirmjäger Panzer-Division 'Hermann Göring' at practice with their Panzerselbstfahrlafette I für 7,62 cm Pak 36(r) (Sd.Kfz.132) "Marder II". The breech block is of the vertical drop type. Affixed to the rear superstructure is the engine crank.

The Marder II was created by combining the chassis of the obsolete Flammpanzer II Ausf. D and Ausf. E with a Russian 7,62 cm F-22 Model 1936 divisional field gun. These captured weapons were available in greater supply than the similar Pak 39 or Pak 40. A total of 1,216 Marder II were built.

10,5cm Le FH 18/2 auf Fahrgestell Pz.Kpfw. II (Sf) (Sd.Kfz. 124). A total of 682 of these vehicles, based on Pz.Kpfw. II Ausf. F chassis, were built by FAMO.

The schwere Infanteriegeschütz 33 (infantry gun) auf Fahrgestell Pz.Kpfw. II (Sf). Based on a lengthened and widened Pz.Kpfw. II chassis, only twelve were produced and were deployed exclusively to North Africa.

because of the limitations of the tank-building industry in Germany. To mount the 105 cm light field howitzer of the German Army, the obsolete Panzer II had to be used again, continuing the usual makeshift pattern. Designed by Alkett and built mainly by Famo of Breslau and an occupied tank factory in Warsaw, Poland, 682 of these vehicles were built during 1942 and 1943. Called "le. FH. 18/2 auf Fahrgestell Pz. Kpfw. II (Sf) (Sd. Kfz. 124) Wespe", they comprised the main equipment of Panzerartillerie units together with the 15 cm "Hummel". Vehicles without guns were used as ammunition carriers under the designation "Munitions Selbstfahrlafette auf Fahrgestell Panzer II". One hundred fifty-eight vehicles were built and could easily be converted to gun carriers, if needed.

Infantry and Panzergrenadier units received limited numbers of "15 cm sIG 33 auf Panzerkampfwagen II", in replacement of the Panzer I based vehicle. They were now considerably lower and much better suited for their intended purpose. Armor protection left much to be desired. Constant mechanical breakdowns, because of the overloading of the chassis, led finally to an enlargement of the chassis. One additional bogie wheel was added on either side, causing renewed difficulties with steering and maneuverability. Very few of these vehicles were actually built.

The proven reliability of the Czech Praga 38 (t) chassis benefited a substantial number of SP conversions, which were in use until the end of the hostilities in Europe. Parallel to the development using Panzer II chassis, an order for a tank-destroyer vehicle using captured Russian guns and Panzer 38 (t) chassis was issued in December of 1941. The chassis remained unchanged, the superstructure altered to receive the gun mount for the Russian weapon. Known as "Panzer Selbstfahrlafette 2 für 7.62 cm Pak 36 (Sd. Kfz. 139)", the vehicles also carried the designation "Marder III". Production started in Prague in March of 1942. A total of 344 units were completed by the end of the year. The limited number of available Russian guns and the availability of the 75 mm Pak 40/3 initiated an order from the Ordnance Department in May of 1942. Again, the 38 (t) chassis was to be used, but this time with a modified superstructure. The basic power train was to be retained. This made these vehicles top-heavy and complicated their maintenance. A large number of these vehicles were issued to anti-tank units during 1942 and 1943 and were known as "7.5 cm Pak 40/3 auf Sfl. 38 (Sd. Kfz. 138)". Starting in March of 1943, a much-improved version of the "Panzerjäger 38 (t) mit 7.5 cm Pak 40/3 (Sd. Kfz. 138)" went into production. They had the engine compartment moved toward the center of the vehicle, received a ballistically much-improved frontal plate, and a clearly-arranged fighting and gun platform. A total of 799 units were built of both versions when their production was terminated in May of 1944. Their task was taken over by the "Jagdpanzer 38 - Hetzer".

Only the heavy infantry howitzer, in great demand for the support of Panzergrenadier units, was mounted on the Czech chassis as standard issue. Developed by Alkett and mass-produced by the Ceskomoravska Kolben Danek of Prague, the vehicle carried the official designation: "sIG 33 (Sfl) auf Panzerkampfwagen 38 (t) (Sd. Kfz. 138/1)". Similar to the AT SP Development, the first version carried the armament forward of the engine compartment, while the final model had the fighting compartment at the rear section of the vehicle. Three hundred seventy units were produced by 1944. Vehicles without armament were again used as ammunition carriers. Their total production amounted to 102. It was contemplated to replace these vehicles with a unit mounting the 15cm sIG on the "Hetzer". This program, however, never materialized.

The constant cry for better protection against allied fighter bombers resulted in the construction of 162 "Flakpanzer 38 (2 cm) (Sd. Kfz. 140)". Built also by CKD, their armament, consisting of only one 2 cm Flak 38, soon proved to be

Panzerjäger 38(t) für 7,62cm Pak36(r) (Sd.Kfz.139). A total of 344 of these vehicles were built, mounting the Russian 7,62cm gun rechambered to accept Pak40 cartridges.

15cm sIG 33/1 auf Selbstfahrlafette 38(t) (Sf) Ausf. M. A spring-loaded flap covers the opening underneath the weapon. A total of 370 units were built and distributed amongst schwere Infanteriegeschütz companies of armored infantry regiments.

The gun shield was of only 15mm thickness; however, the advantage of the design was considered its low silhouette. A few of these units were captured after the second Battle of El Alamein and resurfaced with the Egyptians during their conflict with Israel in 1948.

The self-propelled artillery vehicle 15cm schweres Infantrie Geschütz 33 (Sf.) auf Fahrgestell Panzer II. These furnished the 707 and 708 sIG Kompanien of six units each in North Africa, 1942.

A collaborative design and production effort created the Leichte Feldhaubitze 18/2 auf Fgst. Pz. Kpfw. II (Sf.) (Sd.Kfz. 124). The firm of MAN developed the chassis, Alkett the superstructure, and Rheinmetall-Borsig the weapon. Italy, 1943.

Prototype of the 10,5 cm l.FH. 18/2 für "Wespe" with weapon at maximum elevation of +42°. Note the experimental muzzle brake, which was later streamlined to a rounded design. The driver's compartment became more developed with additional vision slits and rain guards. The range of the artillery piece was 10,675 meters.

"Wespe" brought mobile firepower to the artillery arm and proved greatly effective. Here, vehicles of Grossdeutschland make their operational debut at Kursk, 1943. Typically, a total of six howitzers were provided per battery, and five batteries composed an Abteilung (battalion).

Using the basic Pz.kpfw. 38(t) chassis, Alkett was able to convert 90 vehicles in early 1943. These models were designated Ausf. H for "Heckmotor" (rear-engine), as the powerplant was left in the original location. Placing the sIG 33 at the front, however, overburdened the suspension and the overall design would be changed once more.

15cm schweres Infantrie Geschütz 38 (Sd.Kfz. 138/1) Ausf. K "Grille". Canvas tarps were the only protection for the crew and equipment from the elements. Heat from the engine compartment, however, was brought into the crew space via a small duct.

The Ausf. K model of the 15 cm sIG 33 "Grille" featured a mid-mounted engine compartment. Together with the placement of the fighting compartment at the rear, the center of gravity was balanced about the middle of the vehicle. A total of 282 of these vehicles were produced in two production runs ending in September 1944.

Several 15cm sIG Gesch.Wg. Ausf. H "Grille" served with 38. Pz. Schwere Infateriegeschütz attached to 2. Panzer Division. This example was captured during service in Normandy.

218

The heavy weight of the Russian 7,62cm Pak 36(r) dictated the amount of armor that could be placed on the converted vehicle. Less than 1-ton was added so the performance was maintained. Total weight was 10,670 kilograms.

With a fuel tank capacity of 218 liters, a cross-country range of 140km could be achieved. About 185km range was expected on surface roads.

The basic chassis of the Pz.Kpfw. 38(t) was largely unmodified for use as the Panzerjäger, only the turret and a portion of the upper superstructure were removed. The crew had very little armor protection, with simple tube steel seats and a metal basket to protect them from the muffler.

Panzerjäger 38(t) für 7,62cm Pak 36(r) (Sd.Kfz.139). Mounting the 800kg ma[in]
weapon directly over the Pz.Kpfw. 38(t) base hull resulted in a tall profile of 2[.5]
meters. The Praga EPA engine was increased in horsepower to handle t[he]
additional weight over the original vehicle. A small crew compartme[nt]
permitted a traverse of just 21° in either direction. In total 363 units we[re]
created and contributed their firepower to the battles in Russia and North Afric[a.]

From left to right: Panzerjäger 38(t) für 7,5cm Pak40 Ausf. H (Sd.Kfz. 1[38])
Marder III, 15cm sFH 13/1 (Sf) auf Geschützwagen Lorraine Schlepper
(Sd.Kfz. 135/1), Panzerjäger 38(t) für 7,62cm Pak36(r) (Sd.Kfz. 139) Mar[der]
III. They are photographed while still in storage at the APG museum [at]
Aberdeen in the 1960s.

7,5cm Pak 40/3 auf Panzerkampfwagen 38(t) Ausf. H (Sd.Kfz. 138). The Pz.Kpfw. 38(t) chassis kept the engine in the original rear location. Typically, 38 rounds were carried for the main weapon. This example was formerly of 1.Panzer Division on display in Munster, 1968.

A Russian field gun, rechambered to accept German Pak 40 ammunition, equipped the Panzerjäger 38(t) für 7,62cm Pak 36(r) (Sd.Kfz.139). A German muzzle brake was also added.

Served by a crew of four, the 417 units of Panzerjäger 38(t) Ausf. H took a heavy toll of allied armor even when considered as an interim solution antitank weapon. The concept of the Panzerjäger was refined to a high degree by the end of the conflict.

221

Armed with the venerable 7,5 cm Pak 40/3, the Pz. Jag. 38 Ausf. M (Sd.Kfz. 138) combined the reliable chassis of the Pz.Kpfw. 38(t) with a proven weapon. It was more refined than earlier Panzerjäger with a lower silhouette, mid-mounted engine and balanced center of gravity. This example is seen post war at Aberdeen Proving Ground during the years the collection was stored indoors.

A horizontal tube steel bar served as a stiffener for the superstructure. A pair of rods projecting from the upper sides provided support for a canvas tarp covering. The perforated sheetmetal guard prevented contact with the heated muffler. Armor thickness of the hull sides and rear was 10mm.

Between April 1943 and May 1944, a total of 975 Pz. Jag. 38 Ausf. M were produced. They served on all fronts and their firepower and mechanical reliability proved strong points in the field. This was especially so when employed defensively where lack of armor was less of a hindrance.

Panzerjäger (7,5 cm Pak) auf Sf. 38(t) "Marder" (Sd.Kfz. 138)

Panzerjäger 38 für 7,5cm Pak 40/3 Ausf. M (Sd.Kfz. 138). While the basic design of the Pz.Kpfw. 38(t) chassis was retained, several refinements were incorporated. The hull sides, for example, were extended to the front to form tow points and the engine moved to the center for improved balance. Nevertheless, the Jagdpanzer 38(t) Hetzer, providing an enclosed fighting compartment and improved armor, replaced the entire Marder III series.

2cm Flak 38 L/55 auf Selbstfahrlafette 38(t) (Sd.Kfz. 140).

Aufklärungspanzer 38t (Sd.Kfz. 140/1) mounted a KwK 38 L/55 and coaxial MG42. The hexagonal Hängelafette 38 turret was used in many German reconnaissance vehicles.

inadequate and production ran only from October, 1943, through the Spring of 1944.

A little-known version of this vehicle was the reconnaissance tank 38, or "Aufklärungspanzer 38 (t) (Sd. Kfz. 140/1)". Seventy of these units were built in 1943 and mounted the turret of the standard four-wheel armored car (Sd. Kfz. 222) on a normal 38 (t) chassis. A 2 cm KwK 38 and one MG 34 was provided.

Thoughts were given toward the end of the war to utilize the "Hetzer" chassis for an AA tank, mounting two 3 cm MK 103/ 38 guns, coupled with two Flak 38. It was rather doubtful whether or not this armament could be usefully deployed because of the limited capacity of the chassis. Only wooden mock-up models were built.

It is interesting to note that no Panzer III chassis were used for any kind of makeshift conversion. Only the Russians converted captured Panzer III in mounting 7.62 cm AT guns on a limited number of vehicles. Starting the long list of conversions using the Panzer IV chassis was the "10.5 cm K 18 auf Panzer-Selbstfahrlafette IV a". Only two prototypes were ordered in May of 1941 to fight the expected heavy tanks built in both England and America. Since the 8.8 cm gun proved to be quite adequate for this job, the project was discontinued.

Krupp of Essen was most active in the creation of armored SP artillery pieces. Their first attempt resulted in a 10.5 cm gun carrier called "1e FH 18/1 (Sf.) auf Gw IV b (Sd. Kfz. 165/ 1)". A shortened Panzer IV chassis, using only three instead of the normal four bogies per side, gave enough of a gun platform for a limited traverse of 70°. Eight of these prototypes were field-tested in 1942. Production never started and in 1943 attempts were made to convert these vehicles to tank-destroyer units.

Leichte Panzerhaubitze 18 auf Geschützwagen III/IV (Sf) was developed to compete with the Krupp Heuschrecke 10. The sole prototype shown here is missing the outer shields that fit around the standard gun shield. Turret armor was 10mm.

The 10,5cm leichte Feldhaubitze 18 could be dismounted and the two wheels (missing) and trails to complete the piece were stowed at the rear.

Rheinmettall-Borsig designed the prototype that was subsequently built at Deutsche Eisenwerke. A spare roadwheel (missing) was stored on the stub extending from each hull side. A portion of the dismounting crane was also stored along the side. Five crewmen serviced the vehicle.

Leichte F.H. 43 (Sf.) "Heuschrecke"

One of three prototype Leichte Feldhaubitze 43 (Sf.) "Heuschrecke 10" designed by Krupp. These experimental weapons platforms introduced the concept of 360° traverse, and of deploying the weapon off the chassis on a pedestal. This would provide many options for tactical use, but increase the unit cost. The Geschützwagen III/IV chassis was used.

Leichte F.H. 18/1 (Sf.) Gw. IVb (Sd.Kfz. 165/1)

10,5cm leFH 18/1(Sf) auf Geschützwagen IVb (Sd.Kfz 165/1). Ten of the Krupp prototypes were tested in Russia with 16. Pz.Div. in 1942/43. Lacking a fully rotating turret, they were not adopted for production.

Krupp also initiated the "Heuschrecke" and "Grille" series and built prototypes in both series, allowing for a 360° traverse for the light field howitzer and gear to dismount the weapon from the vehicle. After removal of the gun, the units were used as ammunition carriers or recovery vehicles. Similar vehicles were designed by Rheinmetall, Daimler-Benz, and Skoda. None of them reached production stage.

It was even contemplated to mount a heavy mortar, namely the 30.5 cm Mörser M 16, on a Panzer IV chassis. Two vehicles were needed to carry this equipment. It never went beyond the blueprint stage. The ever-increasing allied supremacy in the air resulted in a crash program to create effective AA tanks. Despite Hitler's reluctance to authorize such a vehicle, the CKD of Prague built 150 of the "Flakpanzer IV Möbelwagen" in 1943.

The word "furniture van" describes best the appearance of these units, which mounted either the quadruple 2 cm AA gun or the 3.7 cm Flak 43. Armor protection for the crew was afforded only during transport, since the armor plates had to be lowered in combat to allow usage of the guns. A different solution had to be found fast and appeared as the "Flakpanzer IV (2 cm) mit Panzerfahrgestell IV/3 (Wirbelwind)". Built by Ostbau in Sagan/Silesia these vehicles mounted the quadruple 2 cm in a 360° traverse turret. They arrived at the front in December of 1943, and were considered as quite an improvement over the previous solutions. It was supplemented in March of 1944 by the "3.7 cm Flak 43 auf Panzerkampfwagen IV Ausf. J. (Ostwind)". Assembled at the Deutsche Eisenwerke of Duisburg, only 40 of these units reached AA units of the Panzer-Divisions.

One of the greatest disadvantages of the above-mentioned vehicles was their great height and the fact that no overhead protection was afforded to the crew. To eliminate these handicaps, Daimler-Benz AG of Berlin received orders to develop the "leichte Flakpanzer IV (3 cm) Kugelblitz". A

The sole prototype 2cm Flakvierling auf Fahrgestell Panzerkampfwagen IV. It was designed in early 1943 but never entered production with this weapon.

3,7cm Flak 43 auf Selbstfahrlafette auf Panzerkampfwagen IV at the Deutsche Eisenwerke factory. The original prototype with 2cm Flakvierling was converted to this configuration.

229

Flakpanzer IV Ostwind (East Wind) prototype with 3,7cm Flak 43 L/89, considered more powerful than the 2cm Flakvierling. An order for 100 was issued 18 August 1944 to replace 'Wirbelwind'. Turret armor was 16mm with top and bottom sides both at 60° of obliquity. Built on Fahrgestell Nr. 83898.

Between December 1944 and March 1945, forty Ostwind were converted from Pz.Kpfw. IV, and seven more were purpose-built. The turret was nicknamed "Keksdose" (Cookie tin).

Comparison, from left to right, of Flakpanzer "Ostwind", "Möbelwagen", and "Wirbelwind" at the firm of Ostbau Sagan, Silisia.

8,8cm Pak 43/1 (L/71) auf Geschützwagen III und IV (Sf) (Sd.Kfz. 164). Known as Nashorn (Rhinocerous) and later as Hornisse (Hornet). Making their combat debut in the summer of 1943, the Nashorn's armament remained potent through the war.

15cm Schwere Panzerhaubitze auf Geschützwagen III/IV (Sf) (Sd.Kfz. 165). The muzzle brake on the Alkett prototype reduced barrel strain when firing high velocity charges, but was deleted from production.

completely enclosed spherical mounting now carried two MK 103 aircraft guns. After five prototypes were built by DB, production was supposed to commence at the Deutsche Röhrenwerke AG. of Mülheim. The end of the war, however, put a stop to this development.

It was a fact that both the Panzer III and IV chassis were never ideally suited as self-propelled mounts. Since both chassis had achieved a high degree of reliability throughout the years, it was only natural to combine proven components of both vehicles to one chassis. Thus, the "Panzer III/IV" was created, Originally destined to become the standard armored vehicle of the "Wehrmacht", it soon became obvious that its capacity was no longer sufficient. As a self-propelled mount, however, the "Geschützwagen III/IV" was built and used in rather substantial numbers. Developed again by Alkett, production was awarded to the Deutsche Eisenwerke. The first order, dated February, 1942, created an AT SP mount, officially designated as "8.8 cm Pak 43/1 (L/71) auf Fahrgestell Panzerkampfwagen III/IV (Sf)". Sd. Kfz. 164. Despite their inadequate armor protection, these vehicles provided the much-needed mobility for the long-barreled 8.8 cm Pak. By 1944, 473 of these units were assembled at the Teplitz-Schönau factory of the Deutsche Eisenwerke. The arrangement of the driver front plate was changed during production, creating two different models.

Originally called "Nashorn", Hitler's order of February 27, 1944, renamed it "Hornisse". Very similar in outside appearance was the artillery version called "Hummel". Alkett-designed, but built by the Deutsche Eisenwerke of Duisburg, these units carried the designation "15 cm Panzer-Haubitze 18/1 auf Fahrgestell Panzerkampfwagen III/IV (St) (Sd. Kfz. 165)". Prototypes showed the howitzer equipped with a muzzle brake, which was omitted on all production vehicles. They were issued to front units starting in 1943 and were standard equipment until the end of the war. Six hundred sixty-six SP guns were built. These gun-carrying units were

Nashorn were designed by Alkett and produced by Deutsche Eisenwerke in Tieplitz-Schonau. A total of 473 units were produced between February 1943 to March of 1945.

A special chassis was designed by Alkett to mount heavy weapons. Termed "Geschützwagen III/IV", the hull was a hybrid design using components of the Pz.Kpfw. III and Pz.Kpfw. IV. The drive train was largely derived from the Pz.Kpfw III Ausf. J, while the hull and suspension came from Pz.Kpfw. IV Ausf. F.

Because of the heavy weight of the 8,8cm Pak 43/1 L/71, armor protection was minimized. This allowed the total vehicle weight to meet the 24-ton design goal. However, only 24-40 rounds of ammunition could be carried internally and on boxes fitted to the front of the vehicle.

Panzerjäger "Nashorn" of Pz.Jg. Abteilung 519, Russia, winter 1943. Leutnant Albert Ernst commanded a platoon of 1.Komp. of this unit. On 23. December 1943, his Nashorn destroyed 14 Russian tanks near Vitebsk. Only 21 rounds were used, and Ernst was dubbed the "Tiger of Vitebsk." The unit insignia is the head of a roaring lion.

supplemented by 150 ammunition carriers, called "Munition-sträger Hummel". Their conversion to gun mounts could be done in the field.

A preliminary tank production program issued on July 14, 1944, suggested the "Panzer III/IV" chassis as the standard chassis for almost all tank destroyer and self-propelled vehicles. It remained a suggestion.

One of the prototypes leading to the subsequent "Tiger" development was the "VK. 3001 (H)", built by Henschel of Kassel. Only two vehicles were built and later converted to SP mounts, carrying a 12.8 cm AT gun. Rheinmetall-Borsig enlarged the chassis and provided limited armor protection. Called "Selbstfahrlafette 12.8 cm", the first vehicle was delivered in August of 1941. Both units saw action in Russia in 1942, where they were promptly lost in combat.

The introduction of the "Panther" also started a development trend utilizing chassis components of this, new vehicle for SP artillery equipment. Rheinmetall-Borsig received an order for a "12.8 cm K 43 (Sf)" in the Spring of 1942. At the same time, Krupp, also became engaged in developing a similar vehicle. In both cases, the guns were demountable. Investigations were also made of the 15 cm FH 43 on such a chassis. Both Rheinmetall and Krupp again built prototypes. Krupp called their development "Grille", while Rheinmetall adopted its designation "Skorpion". Daimler-Benz, in cooperation with Rheinmetall, concluded this development in 1944, in creating a weapon-carrier vehicle using a shortened "Panther" chassis. In all cases, only wooden mock-up models or soft-steel prototypes were completed. Similar results were obvious in the design of a "Flakpanzer Panther" for the 8.8 cm Flak, which never went beyond the model stage.

To accompany and resupply Hummel batteries, 150 Munitionsträger were built. Tarp hooks line the upper side armor and lifting hooks are on top of the driver's compartment.

Hummel (Bumble-Bee) (Sd.Kfz.165) at the APG. This is a late version with driver/radio operator compartment along the width of the entire hull and protective box over the air intake. A 15cm schwere Feldhaubitze 18/1 is mounted.

Panzerjäger 12,8 cm Kanone 40, auf Sf. (VK 3601)

When the VK. 3001(H) project was abandoned, two of the prototype chassis were selected by Rheinmetall-Borsig for conversion as Panzerjäger platforms. The result was the Panzerjäger 12,8cm Kanone 40 auf. Sf. (VK 3601). Both vehicles saw action in Russia where one was destroyed and the other captured in late 1943, with 22 victory rings on the barrel. The 12,8cm Gerät 40 had been developed since 1936 as a Flak weapon, but in 1939 an anti tank version was sought, given the exceptionally high projectile velocity. The captured vehicle is now on display at the Museum of Armored Forces in Kubinka, Russia.

10,5cm K18 L/52 auf Panzer Selbstfahrlafette IVa. Only two were made and both deployed for Operation Barbarossa with 3. Pz. Div. They were successful, penetrating 111mm of 30° sloped armor at 2,000 meters. The insignia of Pz.Jäg. Abt. 521 is carried.

Designed as bunker destroyers, two 10,5cm K18 L/52 auf Panzer Selbstfahrlafette IVa were built. These prototypes were assigned to Pz.Jäg. Abt. 521 for an attack on Gibraltar, but went to Russia instead.

The final Sturmpanzer IV produced from April 1944, with ball-mounted MG 34 in front hull and modest cupola for the commander.

Sturmgeschütz neuer Art (7,5cm Pak L/48) auf Fgst. Pz.Kpfw. IV (Sd.Kfz. 162). Glacis is 60mm and cast mantle is 80mm thick. Musée des Blindés.

The 15cm StuH 43 L/12 was modified by Skoda. This example at Musée des Blindés has pressed-steel return and road wheels.

Panzermuseum Munster's running Hummel at Panzer Testing Ground "Kohlenbissen", 21 August, 1993. Bundeswehr Panzerwerkstatt (Panzer Maintenance Shop) Kampftruppenschule 2 restored it in 1982.

8,8cm Flak 41 auf Sd.Fgst. From 1944, the longer Flak 41 L/75 was mounted in place of the Flak 37 L/56. Sides lowered for all-round traverse.

In 1941, Krupp received an order for a heavy tank-destroyer on a special chassis. Originally intended to carry the 8.8 cm Pak L/56, the specifications were later changed to the 8.8 cm Pak L/71. Three prototypes were ordered and were to be equipped with the Maybach "HL 90" engine. One chassis was subsequently completed but converted to a Flakpanzer. It mounted the 8.8 cm Flak 37 in a 360° traverse, while the armored side walls of the box-like superstructure were folded down during combat. No production ensued.

To finalize this history of German self-propelled equipment, the "Grille 17/21" has to be mentioned. Krupp again received this order in the Spring of 1942, under the official nomenclature "Gerät 5-1702 (17 cm K 43) (Sfl)". Using "Tiger" components, the vehicle had a total weight of 53 tons. Krupp solved the demands in regard to all-round traverse and demountability to the satisfaction of the Ordnance Department. To facilitate railroad transport, the armored side walls of the vehicle could be moved inwards. The demountability was dropped from the specifications in 1944 and one prototype was under construction and almost completed when the war ended. A very similar design called "Gerät 5-2107", mounting the 21 cm Mortar 18, was also under consideration but never completed.

Krupp produced only three 8,8cm Flak 37 auf Grille 10. Built in late 1942, the prototypes initially carried the Flak 37 L/56.

Sonderfahrgestell Grille 10 was based on Pz.Kpfw IV and Sd.Kfz. 9 components to develop a standard heavy weapons chassis.

15 cm s.Panzerhaubitze auf Fgst. Pz.Kpf. III/IV (Sf.) "Hummel" (Sd.Kfz. 165)

14.12.43.

Lb.1615e

Grille 10 were initially developed as Panzerjäger but instead became anti-aircraft weapons. Elevation ranged -3 to +87 degrees.

One Grille 10 was rearmed with Flak 37 and tested in Italy with Heeres Flakartillerie Abteilung (Sf.) 304, attached to 26. Panzer Division.

240

Jagdpanzer 38(t) "Hetzer" für 7,5cm Pak 39. Restored vehicle at Deutsches Panzermuseum Munster. Main weapon had traverse of 11° right and 5° left, and elevation of –6° and +12°. The compact vehicle was only 217cm high and crewed by four men.

Only the loader sat on the right side of the vehicle, and the three other crewmen sat one behind the other. Top armor plate was 10mm thick. The sides were only 20mm, but their angle increased resilience. The wing-shaped shield held a "Rundumfeuer" (remote control) MG 34.

Jagdpanzer 38 was first issued July, 1944. Frontal armor was 60mm. The cast mantle provided an additional 60mm, and several variations were designed. Plans existed for a rigidly mounted gun.

Late model Hetzer with simplified idler wheel patterns. The exhaust was revised to this shape, replacing an earlier horizontal version.

This impeccably restored Sturmgeschütz III Ausf. G resides at the Military Vehicle Technology Foundation of Jacques Littlefield, Portola Valley, CA.

A base red oxide primer served as the undercoat for most German vehicle paint schemes. The paint has worn away and the primer is visible on the lower hull of this 7,5cm Sturmgeschütz Ausf. G at the Patton Museum.

Panzermuseum Munster houses this Sturmgeschütz III Ausf. G that had served in the Finnish Army.

A large variety of Zimmerit patterns existed. Note the waffle pattern on this 7,5cm Sturmgeschütz 40 Ausf. G at the BWB Koblenz Museum, Germany.

Jagdpanther

Panzerjäger Panther für 8,8cm Pak 43/3 (Sd.Kfz. 173). Frontal armor was 80mm, angled at 55°. This vehicle is of the 2. Kompanie, Schwere Heeres Panzerjäger Abteilung 654.

Jagdpanzer V "Jagdpanther" (8,8 cm Pak) (Sd.Kfz. 173)

The wide crew compartment of the Panzerjäger Panther provided more room than the turreted Panther. Two hatches in the roof and a third at the rear provided ample escape access. Here, the crew sits atop their vehicle at Mailly-le-Camp, France, May 1944. Only the driver remains inside.

Panzermuseum Munster has a restored late model Jagdpanther. The 80mm of frontal armor is inclined 55 degrees.

Jagdpanther (Sd.Kfz. 173) at the BWB Koblenz Museum, Germany.

Panzerjäger V Jagdpanther (Sd.Kfz. 173) Musée des Blindés. Early models carried monobloc 8,8cm Pak 43/3 with the gun mantle welded to the glacis.

Jagdpanzer Elefant

"Ferdinand" Sturmgeschütz mit 8,8cm Pak 43/2 (Sd.Kfz. 184). These vehicles are seen at Nibelungen Werke, April 1943, before their departure to the Russian front and their debut at Kursk. A pair of air-cooled gasoline engines powered two electrical generators, which in turn supplied an electric motor to each track. This propelled the 65-ton vehicle to 30 km/h.

Jagdpanzer Tiger (P) "Elefant" (8,8 cm Pak) (Sd.Kfz. 184)

Jagdpanzer Elefant

In the fall of 1943, about 50 Ferdinands were sent to Nibelungenwerke to receive a hull machine gun, wider tracks, zimmerit coating, and a commander's cupola derived from that of the StuG III.

Ferdinand "714" of s.Pz.Jg.Abt 653, Kursk, July 1943. Despite inflicting heavy losses upon the Russians, the Ferdinand crewmen were unnecessarily vulnerable to infantry attack. In addition, the power to weight ratio was poor. Half of the available Ferdinands were destroyed or abandoned.

Elephant "102" (Fahrgestell Nr. 150040) was attached to 1. Kompanie, s.Pz.Jg.Abt 653, which had 11 Elephant, 1 Panzerbergewagen Tiger(P) and 3 Munitionspanzer III. This Elephant was captured during the fighting at Anzio in early 1944. It was evaluated at the APG, shown with the emblem of Sturmgeschütz-Brigade 232.

251

At drill, a Flakpanzer 38 crew of 1. SS-Pz.Div. "Leibstandarte" mounts their vehicle. A mixture of 2cm armor piercing and explosive shells amounting to over 1,000 rounds were carried. The vehicles were issued to units in Italy and the Western Front.

Böhmisch-Mährischen Maschinenfabrik (BMM), formerly CKD, built the Flakpanzerwagen 38(t) in Prague between November 1943 and February 1944. Armor plate of the 8-sided compartment was 10mm. Most of the plate was riveted in place to an angle iron frame.

Flakpanzerwagen 38(t) were issued January-February 1944 to the Flak detachment of each tank regiment in the Panzer division. They were an interim solution until the Flakpanzer IV became available.

Flakpanzer (38t)

2cm Flak 38 L/55 auf Selbstfahrlafette 38(t) of 12. SS-Pz. Div. "Hitlerjugend". These vehicles were desperately needed and delivered to the Panzer Divisions until more powerful weapons could be provided. The 2cm Flak 38 was effective against strafing aircraft between 500 meters to 1950 meters in altitude.

Panzerflak (2 cm) auf Sf. 38(t) (Sd.Kfz. 140)

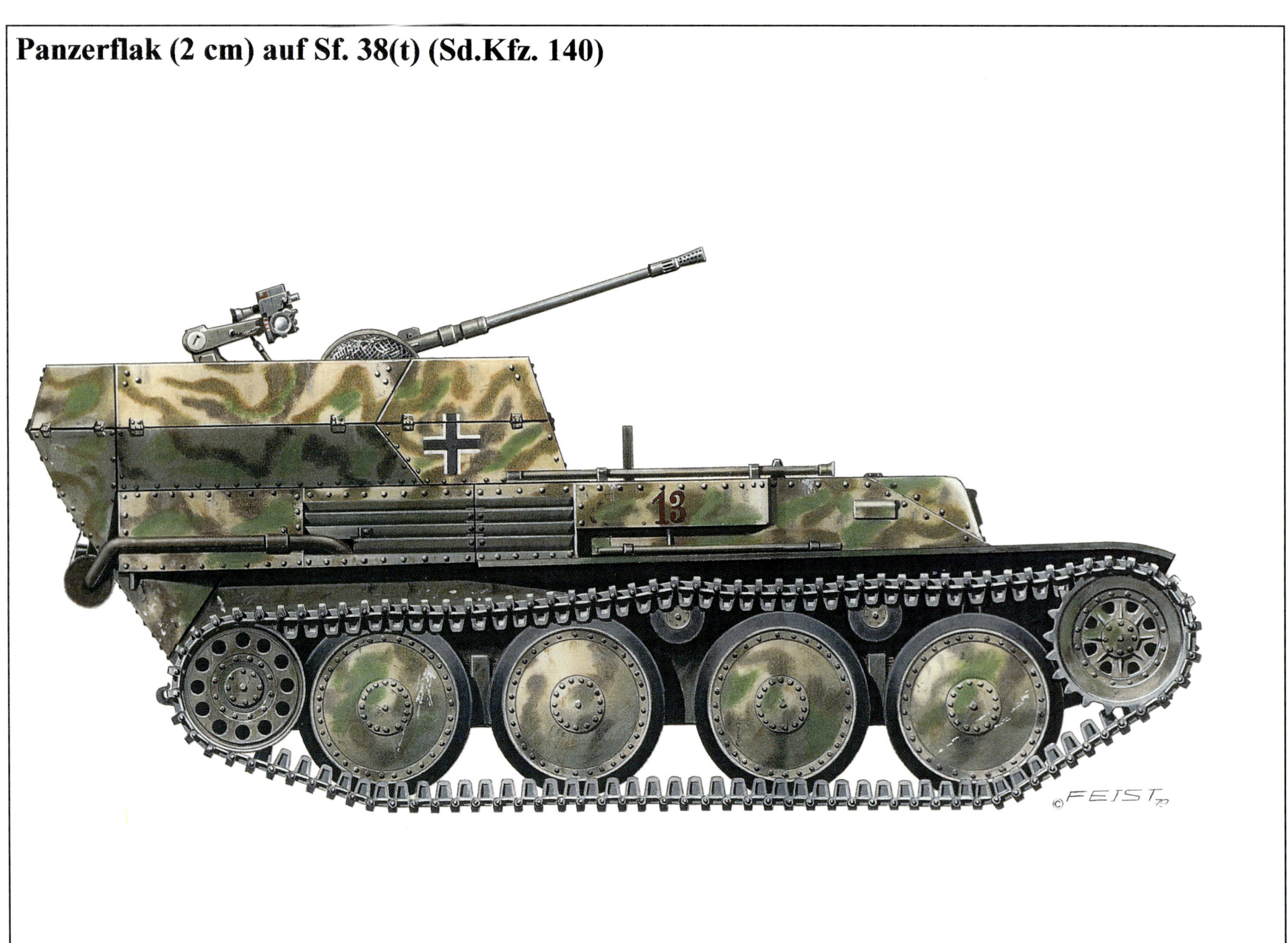

3,7 cm Flak 43 auf Sf. Pz.Kpfw. IV "Möbelwagen"

The 3,7cm Flak 43 fired between 160 and 360 rounds per minute and was fully automatic and gas operated. Eight round clips fed into the tray at left. Muzzle velocity of the 0,7kg shells was 770 meters per second. A total of 320 high explosive rounds and 80 armor-piercing rounds were carried.

Möbelwagen (Sd.Kfz. 161/3). Chassis were provided by Krupp-Gruson and assembly completed by Deutsche Eisenwerke AG. Circular pistol ports allowed defensive fire. This unit, Fahrgestell Nr. 93318, was equipped with 25mm single plate shields.

At practice with the Zeiss Entfernungsmesser 1m R36 stereoscopic rangefinder. Crew consisted of driver, radio operator, gunner, commander and 2 loaders. With corner plates deployed the compartment volume was increased.

Shield specifications varied during production. The first 20 Möbelwagen had double walled shields that were 12mm each. The next 25 were also double walled but 10mm each, and after vehicle 45, single 25mm plate.

One side of the gun shield was shortened and the other side folded, allowing traverse with the side platforms up. Eight of these vehicles were to be issued to each headquarters company of Panzer Regiments stationed on the Western Front. The vehicles were typically issued in groups of four.

Prototype "Möbelwagen", 2cm Flakvierling auf Fahrgestell Pz.Kfw. IV (Sf). An unaltered Pz.Kpfw. IV chassis was fitted with a new wider superstructure and firing platform/shields. Adolf Hitler rejected the 2cm Flakvierling armament, however, and the 3,7cm Flak 43 was substituted. Production commenced in April 1944.

Flakpanzer IV (2cm) mit Fahrgestell IV/3 "Wirbelwind", formerly of SS-Pz.Rgt. 1 with Kampfgruppe Peiper and found by US soldiers on 1 January, 1945.

Ostbau of Sagan built this Wirbelwind on a refurbished Pz.Kpfw. IV Ausf. G chassis, Fahrgestell Nr. 83312. Wirbelwind supplemented the production of other Flakpanzer. In late 1944, 86 units were made. Note the box for the spare barrels and spare radio aerial at rear.

Despite its high rate of fire, the 2cm Flakvierling was arguably less effective than 3,7cm Flak 43 L/89 because the 3,7cm shell had greater stopping power and explosive content.

This Wirbelwind, Fahrgestell Nr. 82853, is built on an early Pz.Kpfw. IV Ausf. G chassis with 50mm front armor. Many gunsights were available for the 2cm Flak 38. This weapon features the Linealvisier 21 device. The large adjustable ring had a horizontal slider at the mounting front and alignment bead at the rear.

A Praga AC/2 engine provided a speed of 30 km/h. The front wheel drive permitted the design to be of a low silhouette. A crew of four was carried on the 11,200-kilogram vehicle, a very low weight considering the firepower it would deliver. Besides the 8,8cm Pak43 L/71, it could also be armed with the 10,5cm leichte Feldhaubitze 18/40/5 L/28.

A traverse of 360° was possible and 34 rounds of ammunition available for the 8,8cm Pak43 L/71. One vehicle saw action in April 1945 near Berlin at Brandenburg with 3.Pz.Jag.Abt. attached to the Infantry Division "Ulrich von Hutten".

In an effort to combine a reliable, standard chassis to carry a range of heavy weapons, the firms of Krupp/Ardelt developed the Leichter Waffenträger für 8,8cm Pak43 L/71. The prototype model, seen here, was to be refined to reach a production goal of 350 units per month by September 1945. Elevation of the weapon ranged from -5° to +42°.

Protype of 8,8cm Pak 43 L/71 auf Sf. Steyr-Daimler- Puch 1945

Prototype of the Waffenträger by Rheinmetall-Borsig/Ardelt with 8,8cm Pak 43 L/71. Despite a semi-enclosed compartment, a lack of strong armor protection was a nominal factor. Germany's late war defensive action allowed for more advantageous use of terrain.

The 8,8cm Pak 43 L/71 was an extremely potent weapon. The shells were fired with a muzzle velocity of over 1000 meters per second, managing to penetrate over 153mm of armor plate at 2000 meters of distance.

SONDERPANZER

Most of the literature dealing with the development of German armor ignores some of the interesting side attempts to create unusual armored vehicles. While these designs never played an important part in the basic concept of armored warfare, they are, nevertheless, significant for their unique approach to certain development problems.

Only limited information about these vehicles is available, since most of them never progressed beyond prototype stage. This chapter will span the wide variety from radio-controlled demolition vehicles, to the futile attempt to create a superheavy tank. The framework of this publication will not allow us to cover all the details of these most interesting designs, but it will, however, undoubtedly clarify many questions which up to now were still shrouded in mystery.

Editor's note: Because the original German specifications and terms used in this book are based on the metric system, the following table is included for convenient referral.

Unit	Abbreviation	Approx. U.S. Equivalent
1 centimeter	cm	0.39 inches
1 kilogram	kg	2.2046 pounds
1 kilopond	kp	2.2046 pounds (not affected by atmospheric pressure)
1 kilometer	km	0.62 miles
1 liter	ltr	1.057 quarts liquid
1 metric ton	t	1.1 tons
1 millimeter	mm	0.04 inches

Panzerkampfwagen VIII Maus, Porsche 205. Prototype mounting 12,8 cm KwK 44 L/55 as main armament with coaxial 7,5cm KwK L/36,5 for use against smaller targets. The inter-locking armor plate was 200mm thick at the glacis, installed at an angle of 55° to an equivalent strength of armor 350mm thick. The nose plate was of the same thickness but installed at an angle of 60°.

Funklenkpanzer

RADIO-CONTROLLED DEMOLITION VEHICLES

Gepanzerter Munitionsträger (VK 301). Designed to accommodate a crew of two and ammunition in the armored boxes at the rear.

Borgward Type "BI" towing mine detonation rollers. The hull was made of concrete so it could be reused. The BI were not used in combat but issued to Minenräum-Kompanie for field testing.

The German Ordnance Dept. issued its first order for vehicles of this nature on October 19, 1939, to the C.F.W. Borgward Co. of Bremen. They were envisioned as full-tracked vehicles, their hull made of concrete, remote-controlled and able to tow a steel roller device. Intended to be sent into enemy mine fields, they were to explode these mines by physical contact. Fifty units of the first prototype, called "B I," were delivered by June of 1940. An improved model, the type "B II", had been ordered in April of 1940 and was now equipped with a Borgward six-cylinder engine, instead of the four-cylinder used on the "B I". These units were officially called "Minenräumwagen Ausf. II (Sd. Kfz. 300)." Production of a batch of 100 units started in July 1940. Intensive field trials pointed out the need for a larger vehicle, which, instead of towing devices to explode mines, could actually deposit a large explosive charge at a given target and return to its base upon receiving an appropriate command via radio. As early as September, 1937, the army had ordered an armored full-tracked ammunition tractor, called "VK 301". Borgward was again responsible for its design. A total of 100 units was to be procured, but constant problems as to their importance delayed their delivery to January 1942, when its production was stopped in favor of the "Ladungsträger RK 4", to be built by Saurer of Vienna. This project also never materialized. Some of the Borgward vehicles served as self-propelled mounts for the 5 cm AT gun and a recoilless rifle. Its main components were used to manufacture the next radio-controlled demolition vehicle, the Borgward type "B IV". These vehicles were ordered in October 1941 and mass production started in April 1942. Ausf. A of this vehicle weighed 3.6 metric tons, while the weight for Ausf. B was

Borgward Type "BII", Minenräumwagen Ausf. II (Sd.Kfz.300). These had a six-cylinder motor of 49 hp but were transported to the battlefield. Once deployed, they were controlled by Kleiner Panzerbefehlswagen I Ausf. B (Sd.Kfz. 265). Just six were produced and used in tests only.

The recoilless 10,5cm Leichtgeschütz L/32 was proposed by Rheinmetall for installation on the VK 3.01 chassis. Only the wooden mock-up was completed using Fahrgestell Nr. B330016.

Panzer Selbstfahrlafette Ia 5cm Pak 38 was an experimental antitank weapon based on the gepanzerter Munitionschlepper VK 302 chassis. The project was abandoned in favor of Panzerjäger with greater firepower.

Panzer Selbstfahrlafette Ia 5cm Pak 38 auf Gepanzerter Munitionschlepper. The spade was deployed to absorb the recoil of the weapon.

increased to 4 tons. Payload in either case amounted to 500 kp. Called "schwerer Ladungsträger" (Sd. Kfz. 301), they came equipped with the Borgward "6 M 2, 3 RTBV" gasoline engine.

The last production batch of Ausf. B was fitted with dry-pin tracks, while all previous issues of the "B IV" vehicle had lubricated, rubber-cushioned track shoes similar to the ones used on half-track tractors. They were followed by Ausf. C, which appeared in 1943 and remained in production until December 1944. They were now fitted with a Borgward 3.8 liter engine, with 78 HP. Increase in armor from 10 to 20 mm brought the total weight to 5 metric tons. They were mainly employed by heavy tank battalions to eliminate obstacles and other hard-to-penetrate defenses.

Another order for a similar, but much smaller vehicle, was received by Borgward toward the end of 1940. It was designated "leichter Ladungsträger" (Sd. Kfz. 302), known also as "Goliath". The first version making its appearance in 1942 was driven by two electric starter motors, was wire-guided, and could carry an explosive payload of 60 kp. They were constructed as cheaply as possible, since these vehicles were blown up with their charge. The electrical version was soon replaced with a similar vehicle propelled with a small two-cycle gasoline engine. Still very small in its outside dimensions, this Ausf. A carried a payload of 75 kp, while an improved version, called Ausf. B, had it increased to 100 kp. Both Zündapp of Nürnberg and Zachertz of Freystadt shared in the production of these "leichter Ladungsträger" (Sd. Kfz. 303). A special two-wheeled cart was used to transport these vehicles. They were never too successful.

By 1944, both the "B IV" series and the "Goliath" were supposed to be replaced by a new vehicle, called "mittlerer Ladungsträger" (Sd. Kfz. 304) or "Springer". Assembled by NSU Werke AG. of Neckarsulm, they utilized components of the motorcycle-half-track tractor, the "Kettenkrad". They

The driver's shields are raised on this Ladungsträger "B IV", Ausf. B (Sd.Kfz. 301) found in Normandy. The vehicle was driven as close as practical to the target, and then remotely controlled for the remaining distance. In front is seen the releasable 500 Kg Sprengladung (explosive charge).

An improved version of the B IV, the Ausführung C, had practically double the armor thickness of its predecessor with 20mm plate on all sides. A more powerful engine was installed to compensate for the added weight.

Near Anzio, Italy, February 1944. Pz.Kpfw. Panther, Ausf. A of 1. Abteilung, 4. Panzer Regiment and 26 Panzer Regiment accompany a Borgward B IV Ausf. B of 301 Funklenk Panzer Abteilung.

Leichter Ladungsträger "Goliath" (Sd.Kfz. 303). Powered by a Zündapp 703cc motorcycle engine, this demolition vehicle carried a charge of up to 100 kilograms. This rear view shows a length of the 650m long spool of internally carried guidance wire.

also had the same 1.5 liter Opel Olympia engine, lightly armored with 10 mm frontal plate, they carried a payload of 300 kp. Their total weight was 2.4 ton. Little is known of attempts during the closing stage of the war to convert some of these units to makeshift fighting vehicles. Called "Kleinpanzer Wanze", they allowed room for only one crew member who did the driving and the shooting with the weapon which was usually a recoilless rifle. Their battle worthiness is highly debatable.

A striking contrast to these small vehicles is provided by the "Räumer S", a gigantic articulated armored mine clearing vehicle weighing 130 metric ton. Only one unit was actually completed by Krupp, Essen. It was supposed to detonate mines by means of its large super-heavy steel wheels. The relatively high ground pressure factor made its use dependent upon terrain and restricted its application severely.

A similar attempt ordered both Alkett and Krupp to design a 40 ton unit, which would be able to clear mine fields with three meter wide passages. Armored and intended to pull steel rollers, it ran under the designation "Maschinelles Minenräumgerät". Not even a prototype was produced.

Krupp "Räumer S". A single prototype was built in 1944. The large wheels were of different widths at front and rear. The 130 ton vehicle could not attempt common battlefield obstacles and the project was dropped.

Minenräumpanzer III prototype produced by Krupp. Minenlaufwerk (Mine rollers) were attached to the forward bulkhead. The suspension was lowered and it was hoped the extra height would add protection against mine blasts.

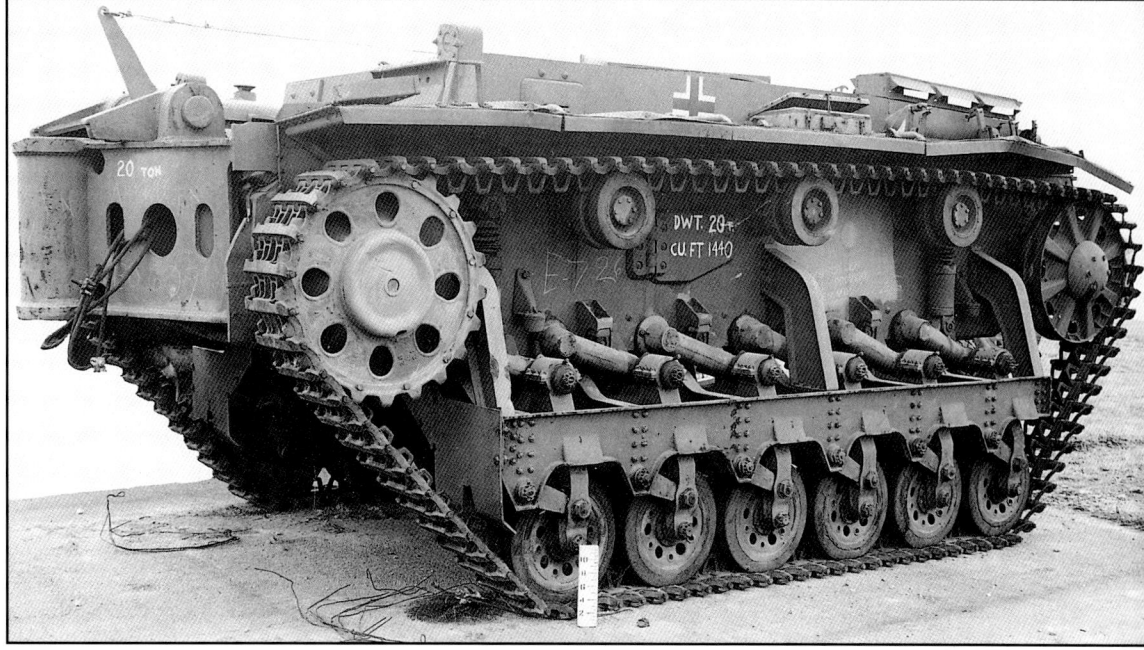

Minenräumpanzer IV mit minenrollen. Front rollers cleared a path for the tracks, while the trailing rollers detonated the mines between the path swept by the front rollers. A Pz.Kpfw. IV Ausf. C was used for these tests.

269

Überschwere Sfl. Artillerie

SUPER-HEAVY SELF-PROPELLED ARTILLERY

The mobility of super-heavy artillery pieces was always of great concern to the German High Command. Already in World War I, their achievements in moving the 42 cm "Bertha" mortar surprised the Allies and allowed the capture of the fortress of Liege in Belgium. Steps to create similar guns were taken as early as 1937 to allow the penetration of heavily-protected places. While normal transport was to utilize the rail system, short distance travel to the firing position was to be accomplished by means of a self-propelled, full-tracked chassis. Only one battery of these units was completed, consisting of six vehicles, with a seventh kept in reserve. It was called "Gerät 040" or "Karl Gerät" and mounted a 60 cm mortar L/8. Its range was only 4500 meters. The vehicle itself weighed 115 metric tons, loaded on two special railroad trolleys, its total weight increased to 180 tons. Two different but similar tracked systems were tried, using torsion bars and allowing the vehicles to be lowered to eliminate any springing action. While the gun and its mount was developed, and built, by Rheinmetall, the engine, a converted aircraft engine, was supplied by Daimler-Benz. Three of the units were equipped with a fuel-injected gasoline engine, type "MB 503", while the rest received a Diesel engine, type "MB 507 C". These power plants were twelve-cylinder "V" units, with a reduced output of 580 HP. To increase the range of the guns to at least 10,000 meters, Rheinmetall received an order in February 1941 to manufacture six barrels of 54 cm bore, ten calibers in length. They were to replace the worn-out 60 cm tubes, the first barrel to be delivered in May 1942. The unit was now called "Gerät 041". Its total weight in firing position was 123 metric tons. All these units saw limited action against Brest-Litowsk and Sevastopol in Russia, where their formidable fire power assisted in the defeat of these heavily-defended places.

Prototype chassis of 60cm Mörser "Karl", (Gerät 040) built in 1939 by Rheinmetall-Borsig. This vehicle had eight road wheels per side; later production vehicles had eleven. The powerplant was a 12-cylinder Daimler-Benz motor yielding a speed of about 10 km/h. A total of 1,200 liters of fuel were carried.

Nicknamed "Thor", the 54cm Mörser (Gerät 041) was issued to 833. schwere Artillerie Abteilung (mot.) along with three other self-propelled mortars of its kind. The longer 54cm barrel provided an additional 5,500m of range.

270

In 1941, similar self-propelled guns were ordered by Waffen-namt from both Krupp and Rheinmetall. Krupp received its order in January to use the railroad gun K 5 (E) for this purpose. This 28.3 cm gun had a total weight of 160 tons. One was ordered but never completed. Rheinmetall made similar arrangements for the 24 cm gun K 4, giving it a total weight of 122 tons. In both cases, the tracked chassis was very similar to the one used for the "Karl Gerät". Krupp also investigated the feasibility of transporting this heavy contraption between two "Tiger" chassis to provide greater mobility. No production ensued.

The suspension of Gerät 041 "Thor" has been lowered in preparation for firing. This eliminated the strain on the chassis. For the 54cm barrel, a 1,580kg heavy charge was developed. This round traveled at 380m/s with a maximum range of 10,000 meters. The propellant charge itself weighed 57kg.

271

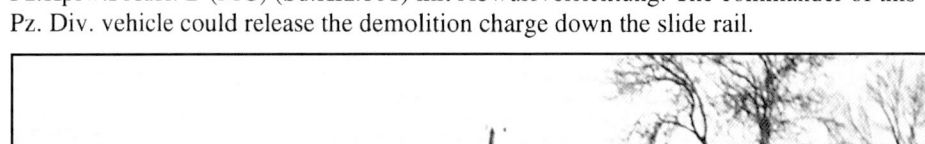

Approximately 100 Ladungsleger I were completed in time for the campaign in France. The arm extended 2.75 meters from the rear.

Pz.Kpfw.I Ausf. B (MG) (Sd.Kfz.101) mit Abwurfvorrichtung. The commander of this 7. Pz. Div. vehicle could release the demolition charge down the slide rail.

Another Ladungsleger I design used a cable-operated arm to drop the charge in place. A contract dated May 9, 1940 was given to Waggonfabrik Talbot of Aachen to build these vehicles, which were issued to Panzer-Pionier-Kompanien.

272

Ladungsleger I

Ladungsleger I with 7. Pz. Div. practices with the 50kg charge. It was difficult to place in tough defenses without losing the light vehicle.

Panzerkampfwagen II (Fl.) (Sd.Kfz. 122)

Pz.Kpfw. II (Fl) of 19. Panzer Division. Each of the two Flammenwerfer Anlagen (Flamethrower nozzles) could rotate 180° and elevate between -10° and +20°. Enough fuel for 80 blasts of 2-3 seconds each was carried. Maximum range was 25 meters.

One MG 34 was mounted in the turret for suppressing fire. The commander had excellent vision from the large vision ports. Smoke grenade launchers are mounted to either side at the rear.

Pz.Kpfw. II (Fl) suffered heavily because of the thin armor protecting the fuel. All surviving vehicles were converted to Panzer Selbstfahrlafette 1 für 7,62cm Pak36(r) (Sd.Kfz. 132).

Four large boxes to either side held the tanks of compressed nitrogen propellant. This propelled the blasts of Flammöl, contained in two, 100-liter tanks within the armored hull. Only the commander's hatch provided entry.

Sturmgeschütz III (Fl). Between May-June 1943, about 10 StuG III Ausf. F/8 that had been returned for repair were fitted with the 1,4cm Schwade flamethrower system. All ten were used for training and later refitted with 7,5cm StuK 40 L/48 in January 1944.

Each of the two Flammenwerfer Anlagen (Flamethrower nozzles) could rotate 180° and elevate between -10° and +20°. Enough fuel for 80 blasts of 2-3 seconds each was carried.

The target was first soaked with cold Flammöl. Then an electric Smitskerzen (glow plug) ignited the mixture. This blast lit the cold oil deposit.

Panzerkampfwagen III (Fl.) (Ausf. M) (Sd.Kfz. 141/3)

Pz.Kpfw. III (Fl) Ausf. M (Sd.Kfz. 141/3). Flammpanzer III received an additional 3cm of welded plate to the hull front. This example at APG is Fahrgestell Nr. 77651 and was captured in Italy. It is now at the Wehrtechnische Studiensammlung Museum in Koblenz.

Production of the Land/Wasserschlepper was only 21 units. They were restricted to transportation duties within secured areas.

The department for development and testing Waffen-Prüf 5 conducted trials and was specifically responsible for pioniere (engineer) equipment. Prominent markings such as these were often designed to mislead allied intelligence. These vehicles are of the first production batch of seven.

Rheinmetall-Borsig AG was commissioned to develop a tracked amphibious vehicle in 1936. The Land/Wasser Schlepper (L.W.S.) was tested for potential use in the proposed invasion of England.

Land/Wasserschlepper (LWS)

Between the propellers is the tow hook for a floating trailer with 18t of cargo. The vehicles supplied German units in the Baltic Sea states and used to capture the islands Moon, Ösel and Dagö.

Land/Wasserschlepper (LWS)

This L.W.S. is of the second production run of 14 vehicles. It was crewed by 3 men,
powered by a Maybach HL 108 TR engine and could carry 20 passengers.

Panzerfähre (Pz.F.)

Panzerfähre (Pz.F.). Klöckner, Humboldt, Deutz AG built only two prototypes of the amphibious vehicles in mid 1942. Designed to replace the Landwasserschlepper, Panzerfähre was armored to withstand rifle bullets. A pontoon would fit between two vehicles, allowing loads up to 24 tons to be ferried across rivers and lakes.

Bergepanzer 38 Fahrgestell Nr. 322678, completed at BMM in February 1945. The spade with winch was introduced to Bergepanzer production the same month.

Bergepanzer 38 carried a collapsible 2t tubular crane, a winch, and a spade. Only vehicles of equal weight could be towed without harming the powertrain, but this was often ignored in emergencies.

Instandsetzungsfahrzeug 38(t). Removing the turrets from older model Pz.Kpfw. 38(t) created Instandsetzungsfahrzeug (Repair vehicles) as well as Munitionspanzer.

Bergepanzer 38

A captured Bergepanzer 38 was taken to APG for evaluation after the war, but was scrapped for the Korean War effort.

Bergefahrzeug 38

The tracked Bergefahrzeug 38(t) carried mechanics to the location where a vehicle needed to be repaired in place and could not be retrieved otherwise.

Bergefahrzeug 38(t) were based on retired Pz.Kpfw. 38(t) by removing the turret and used as workshop vehicles. Here, its crane removes the 7,5cm KwK tank gun of a Pz.Kpfw. IV Ausf. G.

Bergepanther Ausf. A recovery vehicle at Kummersdorf training ground. This late pattern spade design prevented it from sinking too deep when set in soft ground. Note the 2cm KwK 38 along with MG 34 in Fliegerbeschußgerät (anti-aircraft) mounting.

This Bergepanther Ausf. D is pulled by another tow vehicle as it retrieves the Panther behind it. Very soft ground threatened mechanical damage to even Bergepanther if unassisted. The wood beam along the hull was used when pushing other vehicles.

Demand for recovery vehicles was so high that MAN delivered 12 turretless Pz.Kpfw. V Panther Ausf. D in June 1943 as stopgap recovery tanks. They had no specialized recovery equipment and served with s.Pz.Jg.Abt. 653.

Bergepanther Ausf. A, Fahrgestell Nr. 212161 built by Henschel, September 1943. Use of the spade doubled pulling power. Bergepanther could lift engines and transmissions with the 1,5t crane installed. The cable of the 40-ton winch passed through the guide assembly of four steel rollers, preventing it from wandering across the engine deck.

The pair of square metal plates at hull front was used to attach a wooden beam when pushing a disabled vehicle. Reinforcing gussets kept these plates from failing under load. The beam prevented the Bergepanther tracks from hitting the vehicle being pushed.

Many Bergepanther tended to ride nose high due to the removal of the heavy turret and gun. Fuel capacity was 1,075 liters.

286

Bergepanther

The fighting compartment, main armament and frontal extra armor plates were removed and only a small single MG 34 was provided.

Five Panzerbergewagen Tiger (P) were produced by August of 1943 to assist in recovery of the 65 ton Elephants. A minimal crew compartment allowed the trade of weight for towing power. Three vehicles were delivered to s.Pz.Jg.Abt. 653.

Timber beams were carried for recovery assistance. A crane, not shown, was attached at the support brackets seen on each side.

The superstructure of this Bergepanzer III was removed to reduce overall weight, which augmented the towing capacity.

This Pz.Kpfw. III Ausf. J has been converted to a Bergepanzer III recovery vehicle. Holes are cut in the Panzerschürzen to allow for access to equipment stored on the fender. Beginning January 1944 all Pz.Kpfw. III returned for overhaul were converted to Bergepanzer, and production reached 150 by December 1944.

Removal of the turret was mediated by a circular canvas tarp. A length of track with Ostketten has been stored at the hull front.

Munitionsträger für Gerät 040

Munitionsträger auf Panzer IV carried four shells and charges for the 60cm Mörser Karl-Gerät 040. To lift the shells, it was equipped with a gasoline-electric motor driven Wippkran 2,5t crane. It is seen here in the stored position.

Rheinmetall built this Munitionsträger IV in August 1941 on the Pz.Kpfw. IV Ausf. F chassis.

Electrical power for the crane was provided by the same 2-cylinder gasoline motor/generator used in a normal Pz.Kpfw.IV to drive the electrical motor for turret traverse.

Munitionspanzerwagen IV für 54 u. 61,5 cm Mörser "Karl und Thor".

The superstructure of the Pz.Kpfw. IV Ausf. F was completely redesigned. Braces on the front hull held a Geschossgreifer shell gripping device (missing). In the storage compartment, metal straps with wood absorbers secured the rounds. This example was scrapped during the Korean War.

291

60 cm Mörser "Karl" (Gerät 040)

Mörser "Karl" Nr. III of 833. Schwere Artillerie Abteilung engaging the fortress at Brest Litowsk, June 1941. With the assistance of the Munitionsträger, a 60 cm shell could be fired every 10 minutes. Elevation was 0° to +70°, and 4° traverse either side.

Pz.Kpfw. I Ausf. A converted to a workshop recovery vehicle of 3. Panzer Division.

Chassis used for training by the NSKK (National Socialist Motor Corps).

Infantry carrier based on Pz.Kpfw. 1 Ausf. A.

Brückenleger Pz.Kpfw. II Ausf. B. Magirus created a bridgelayer with a two-piece sliding bridge. These are with engineers of 7. Pz. Div., Belgium, 1940.

Pionierpanzerwagen III. Beginning in 1943, some Pz.Kpfw. III were modified from Pz.Kpfw. III Ausführung L and Ausf. M by removing the turret and adding racks for engineering equipment.

These Pionierpanzerwagen III bring lumber to stabilize temporary bridges.

Two Panzerkampfwagen IV Ausf. D were the basis for the Krupp-designed Schnellbrücke (fast bridge). Designated Brückenleger IV b, the vehicles were assigned to Panzer-Pionier-Batallion 39 of 3. Panzer Division. France, May 1940.

A Magirus Brückenleger based on the early Pz.Kpfw. III Ausf. A chassis. Seen on its own bridge, the support girders over the superstructure carried the platform.

Twenty Brückenleger IV' b were completed in April 1940. By combining the platforms from several vehicles, the BL IV could ascend taller obstacles. The gantry lifts another section into position.

All four Krupp Brückenleger IV c participated in the invasion of Russia. These vehicles slid the bridge horizontally to span the distance. The heavy sections could be broken down into three payloads so the BL IV and support trucks could travel at the same speed.

Artillery support and anti-aircraft defense are efficiently combined in the Artillerie-Flakwagen car designed for the Standard-Panzerzug Type BP42 (Bahn-Panzer 42) armored train. Note the rising sun emblem of Armored Train No. 63. The different cars were repeated symmetrically on either side of the centrally located locomotive and tender.

Bahn-Panzer 42 (armored train 42)

Armored Train No. 24 carried an infantry detachment of 125 men. On the nearest car is one Gb.Kan.15 (ö/t) L/28 7,5cm gun and one 2cm Flak 38.

Infantry and command cars of Armored train No. 24. The main armament was supplemented by a series of rifle and machine gun ports, shown here with MG34. Thirteen of these weapons were carried.

Standard-Panzerzug Type BP42 carried a pair of Kommandowagen (Command car). They held intelligence and medical troops and part of the infantry unit. In the middle is an observation post with a searchlight and a frame antenna for the radio system.

Flakwagen mit 2cm Flakvierling 38. The flak crews were largely exposed. Seen practicing, the gunner looks on while the sight-gunner adjusts the range. The crew consisted of five, the gun commander and four gunners. The K1, or gunner, aimed the weapon and operated the trigger pedals after the order to fire was given. The K2, or sight-gunner, set the ranges called out by the rangefinder operator on the sight. The K3 observed the target, estimated its direction of flight and any changes in altitude, and set these on the sight. The K4, or ammunition bearer, loaded the magazine, changed clips and emptied shell casings.

This view is taken from the artillery end of the Artillerie-Flakwagen car, showing the central command and control area. The 2cm Flakvierling 38 could be depressed as much as −10° and elevated +100 degrees. High explosive shells traveled close to 900 mps. Against armored targets, the 2cm Pzgr Patr 40 L'spur ("Leuchtspur" or bright ignition tracer) was developed with a tungsten core penetrator capable of defeating 40mm of armor at 100 meters. The limited supplies of tungsten, however, meant that few rounds were available.

Artillerie-Flakwagen carried a variety of weapons. This car of Panzerzug 63 features the 7,62 cm Feldkanone 295 l/(r). Other cars of the same type carried the Polish 10cm leichte FH 14/19(p) or German 10,5 leichte FH 18 M. Panzerzug 63, commissioned in October of 1942, was assigned first to Heeresgruppe Nord, 18. Armee and fought there until April of 1944 and transferred to Heeresgruppe Süd. Despite its heavy armament, it was destroyed on 17 July 1944 outside the central rail depot town of Krasne, in Eastern Galicia.

Offensive capability was enhanced by the placement of Pz.Kpfw. 38(t) in specially designed railcars for the BP 42/44 armored train.

Artilleriewagen with weapon to one side carried an infantry compartment on the other. Previous designs placed an artillery piece on both sides of the car, but one was later deleted to prevent the loss of both if the car was destroyed. A similar car was located on the opposite end of the train.

Standard platform cars with repair equipment were often placed in front of the Panzerträgerwagen. It is shown carrying the road wheels for the Panhard 38(f) scout car ahead of it.

Schwerer Spähwagen

The prototype Artilleriewagen mit Pz.IV Turm 7,5cm KwK L/24. These featured their own powerplant and could be used singly or in groups. They were known as schwere Spähwagen (s.Sp. heavy scout cars).

Known as Panzersicherungswagen (armored security wagon), their low weight allowed travel on track of lesser capacity in the Balkans. They were built by Steyr in 1944.

Adolf Hitler inspects a Kommandowagen für Panzerzug (Sp.). Ports for six machine gun stations provided all-round defense.

Armored louvers protect the engine air intake port. Four trains of 10 cars each were deployed in the Balkans in 1944. Automatic central coupling allowed the composition of a train to be quickly modified into individual vehicles or different groups.

To counter the increasing threat from tanks, the Panzertriebwagen with two Pz.Turm IV/H 7,5cm KwK L/48 was designed. A crew of 6 men serviced the car. They are unlikely to have been employed before the war ended. The Americans found this example at the factory in Steyr.

Panzerdraisine Artilleriewagen mit Pz.IV Turm 7,5cm KwK L/24. These provided heavy fire support but were much simpler and lighter than the armored cars of the BP-42/44 series. Deployed in trains of twelve units each, the composition usually consisted of four infantry cars, two command cars, four of these artillery cars with Pz.Kpfw. III Ausf. N or Pz.Kpfw. IV turrets, and two anti-aircraft cars.

Designed in 1944 for Eisenbahn Panzerzug 74, the Panzerjägerwagen mit 7,5cm KwK L/48 carried a plow blade in front.

Unfinished Jagdpanther components are stored at the Maschinenfabrik Niedersachsen GmbH (MNH) Hannover, June 1945.

BIBLIOGRAPHY

Willi A. Boelcke
Deutschlands Rüstung im Zweiten Weltkrieg

Otto Carius
Tiger im Schlamm

Bruce Culver - Uwe Feist
Tiger I, Panther, Schwere Panzer, Tiger I and Sturmtiger in Detail, Panther in Detail.   Ryton Publications

Uwe Feist - Wolfgang Fleischer
Sturmgeschütz   Ryton Publications

Wolfgang Fleischer
Deutsche Panzer 1935-1945

Fritz Heigl
Taschenbuch der Tanks (1926, 1935/38)

E. Johannes
Otto-u. Dieselmotoren, ihre Eignung für militärische Kraftfahrzeuge

Robert Johnson
Hummel   Ryton Publications

K. Kaufmann
Panzerkampfwagenbuch

Hartmut Knittel
Panzerfertigung im Zweiten Weltkrieg

Werner Oswalt
Die Kraftfahrzeuge und Panzer der Reichswehr, Wehrmacht u. Bundeswehr.
Motorbuch Verlag

Karl Pawlas
Waffen Revue, Nr. 1 - 100

W. Regenberger
Panzerfahrzeuge-u. Einheiten der Ordnungspolizei 1936-45

Walter Spielberger -Uwe Feist
Aero-Armor Series, Volume 1 - 13   Aero Publishers

Walter Spielberger
Militärfahrzeuge Band: 2,3,5,7,8,9,11,13,14 and 15
Motorbuch Verlag

Walter Spielberger - Friedrich Wiener
Die deutschen Pz.Kpfw.III und IV mit ihren Abarten 1935-45

F.M. von Senger und Etterlin
Die deutschen Panzer 1926 - 1945

G. Tornau - F. Kurowski
Sturmartillerie

Friedrich Wiener
Gepanzert auf Strasse und Schiene

Heinrich Wüst
Kraftfahrzeugtechnik des Kampfpanzers

DIENSTVORSCHRIFTEN

RYTON PUBLICATIONS
P.O. Box 2306, Bellingham, WA 98227

Panzerspähwagen

New!

Uwe Feist and Robert Johnson

Panzerspähwagen (armored scoutcar) is the title of Ryton Publication's latest release.

All the variations of the German four wheeled armored car are represented in 152 pages with over 280 color- and black and white photographs. The Sd.Kfz. 223, 260 and 261 series vehicles are illustrated with color sideviews by Uwe Feist.

The hardbound 9" x 12" book, 152 pages and 288 photos is printed on high quality art paper in the usual Ryton format.

Retail price: $ 45.00